The Beatitudes

When Mountain Meets Valley

The Beatitudes

When Mountain Meets Valley

By Ron Dart

FRESH WIND PRESS

Edited by Kevin Miller (www.kevinwrites.com)
Cover design by Brad Jersak (www.bradjersak.com)
Front cover and author photos by Kevin Miller
Printed in Canada by Friesens, Altona, MB (www.friesens.com)

Library and Archives Canada Cataloguing in Publication

Dart, Ron Samuel
The Beatitudes : when mountain meets valley / by Ron Dart

Includes bibliographical references.
ISBN 0-9733586-8-8

1. Beatitudes. 2. Christian Ethics. 3. Christian Life I. Title.

BT382.D37 2005   241.5'3

C2005-905027-6

Fresh Wind Press
2170 Maywood Court
Abbotsford, BC, Canada
V2S 4Z1

www.freshwindpress.com

Contents

Dedication

To Karin, as always,
mountain watcher, friend, fellow pilgrim, fine wife,
and contemplative "peak bagger."

Ich liebe dich.

Preface

Books in the running brooks,
Sermons in stones,
Good in everything.
                    William Shakespeare

We had the experience, but missed the meaning.
                    T. S. Eliot

For many decades, I have spent a great deal of time near tarns, hiking across talus slopes, rambling along rock rims, and walking to and fro along mountainsides. Many have been the overnight stay under a hunter's moon in lookouts bolted tight onto rock slabs on peaks high above snow, scrub, alpine meadow, and tree line. My wife and I actually met in the mountains in 1975, and we were married at the base of Crow's Nest Mountain (the first mountain we climbed together) in 1978. Mountain flowers were aplenty, and glacier lilies graced us with their bright yellow presence as bride and groom came through a copse of greening trees.

Mountain meadows, highlands, rock crags, and peak life in general offers a perspective on the hurly burly and whirligig of time in the valley that lowland life often obscures. As soothing as trips to the peaks can be though, there is always a temptation to turn such journeys into hasty jaunts. Those who dash up paths, round switchbacks, find the peak, and then hasten back down again miss much. As Eliot notes in the quote above, they have an experience, but they miss the layered and multiple meanings hidden within the hike. The streams and brooks are ancient books. The stones and slopes have sermons to preach. The landscape we traverse will, if heeded well, mirror an inner landscape (or "inscape," as poet Gerard Manley Hopkins called it).

Just as there are solid mountains, transient clouds, seasonal flowers, rushing and dry streams, bright and turbulent weather, and shady forests in the outer life and landscape, the same things exist in the inner life or inscape. The hidden languages of landscape and inscape are there for those who have eyes to see and ears to hear. But to see and hear in a wise and insightful way, we must allow a more meditative way of knowing to nudge aside our tendency to rush from one insight to the next, like a hiker eager to "bag" the next peak. A more contemplative way of being must question a more distracted and off-centre way of life.

Martin Heidegger was one of the most important philosophers in the 20th century. His *Memorial Address* and *Conversation on a Country Path About Thinking* point the way to doing philosophy and theology in a more contemplative and meditative way. Heidegger often went to his cabin in Bavaria to listen deeper, to explore his inscape. Heidegger's turn to a more contemplative way must be welcomed, although the content of such a hearing and notion of being should also be questioned. Many of the American Beats from the 1920s–1950s (Kenneth Rexroth, Gary Snyder, Philip Whalen, and Jack Kerouac) lived on mountaintops for a period of time as forest fire lookouts. Such a meditative and contemplative turn signaled a firm "No!" to the frantic, active life, the Protestant work ethic, and Willy Loman's bad dream of the USA. This tale is well told by John Suiter in *Poets on the Peaks: Gary Snyder, Philip Whalen & Jack Kerouac in the North Cascades* (2003). I have also spent many hours hiking in the North Cascades, including time at Snyder and Whalen's lookout at Sourdough Mountain and Kerouac's lookout on Desolation Peak. This has helped me realize that those who have spent more than two months alone on a lookout know the meaning of contemplation, inner hikes and landscape life. As much as I have valued the insights of the Heidegger and the Beats, *New Seeds of Contemplation* (1961) by Thomas Merton and *Four Quartets* (1943) by T. S. Eliot speak even more powerfully about a meditative and contemplative way of knowing and being.

- Solitude by choice

Jesus went up b/c he knew he was going to die

No stranger to contemplation, Jesus also went up to the mountain often. Like the Beats, he did not go to such heights merely to bag another peak. He was neither so silly nor so shallow. Jesus went to the mountains to get away from the many demands and expectations of valley life. He went to such places of silence to refocus, to re-centre, and to see and hear better and deeper. Jesus knew that if he was to live a genuine, full, and authentic life in the valley, he had to spend a great deal of time up on the mountain. Through his commitment to both peak and valley, Jesus set a powerful example for his disciples and the rest of us to follow.

The spiritually sensitive in the West tend to turn to the East for insight and wisdom. Books such as the *Tao Te Ching, The Heart Sutra, The Diamond Sutra, The Upanishads, Bhagavad Gita, Road to Heaven: Encounters with Chinese Hermits, Poems of the Masters* (translated by Red Pine), and the teachings of Han Shan (of Cold Mountain), Ram Dass Thich Nhat Hanh, and the Dalai Lama have meant much to many. In this turn to the Orient for illumination, the teaching of Jesus in the Beatitudes has often been ignored. However, the Beatitudes contain a sense of depth, maturity, and integrative thought that is often lacking in the texts listed above.

The contemplative tradition within the West tends to define the spiritual journey in three phases: purgative, illuminative, and unitive. This classification tends to ignore the fact that the contemplative journey has substantive political, social, and economic implications as well. Many modern mystics have recognized this failing in understanding and defining the contemplative pilgrimage. That is why a fourth stage has been added: *transformative*. It is seems to me that the Beatitudes embody all four phases: purgative, illuminative, unitive, and transformative. This makes perfect sense, of course. Jesus understood the waymarks of the mature and integrated faith journey, and the Beatitudes best embody such a path between peak and valley.

Jesus did some of his deepest and most significant teachings on the mountain. His most substantive ethical insights are embodied in the Sermon on the Mount and the Beatitudes, both of which were given from on high. The Sermon on the Mount begins with Jesus going up

given on high?

Nurtured in the valley. 11

the mountain and calling his disciples to join him. It was from such a still and quiet place that he imparted that which was nearest and dearest to him. Jesus did not pass on more facts, statistics, information or knowledge. He was more interested in wisdom, insight, awakening, and illumination, with the transformation of the inner and outer being. This commitment to transformation is what the Beatitudes are all about.

The Beat poets of the North Cascades, who lived in solitude as lookouts, were well aware that the use of the term "Beat" was connected to beat down, beat up, in the beat, beatific, and, more to the point, rooted and grounded in the Beatitudes. The more mature Beats were deeply contemplative and committed to the mystical way of the Beatitudes. Likewise, those who have spent time in the mountains and on high rock trails know the importance of well placed cairns and stones upon the path. These cobbled stones, called "rip-rap," on steeper and more slippery rocks make for an easier ascent and descent for both people and animals in the high regions. We can, in many ways, see the Beatitudes as a type of spiritual rip-rap. Like their physical counterparts, the Beatitudes offer our feet firm footing when going up or down treacherous slopes.

This missive is a brief reflection and commentary on the rip-rap steps that make up the Beatitudes. The Beatitudes can tell us much about the deeper meaning of the time-tried path to the eternal peak. They can also ensure that we do not lose our footing as we traverse the slopes where mountain and valley meet.

RSD
Abbotsford, BC
August 2005

Introduction

*At the still point of the turning world. Neither flesh nor
fleshless; Neither from nor towards; at the still point, there the
dance is, But neither arrest nor movement.*
          T. S. Eliot, *Four Quartets* (Burnt Norton)

Shall we follow the deception of the thrush?
          T. S. Eliot, *Four Quartets* (Burnt Norton)

These days are marked by an abiding interest in spirituality. However, when the interest in spirituality does not lead to a passion for justice, it becomes merely a veiled form of narcissism. A hunger for justice also typifies our time. But when the thirst for justice is not shaped by a historically informed notion of wisdom and spirituality, the passion for justice and peace can become a brittle ideology. The Beatitudes, when read rightly and internalized wisely, offer a way out of this dichotomy, a means of growing in inner integrity and living forth the faith journey in a just and peacemaking way.

Another worrisome tendency amongst some of the most sensitive and insightful is to elevate spirituality, mysticism, contemplation, and the wisdom traditions within the West and East while negating or subordinating the role of dogma, justice, peacemaking, and the institutions that bear these political hopes and faith visions. The inner life is held high and sacrosanct while the outer life is regarded as secondary to the "real" spiritual quest. This sort of dualism should alert the more thoughtful that something is not quite right. The "spirituality is good/religion is bad" model fails to see that there is good in religion and problems

13

within spirituality and that such a dualistic paradigm can easily become yet another dogma and institution. Once again, the Beatitudes can and do address such a dilemma, offering a middle way between these two extremes.

The discovery of many Gnostic texts at Nag Hammadi in 1945 has exacerbated our tendency toward dualism. These texts have also raised some important textual questions for many Christians, such as, "Who was the real Jesus, and what did he really say?" Many of the Nag Hammadi texts, including *The Gospel of Thomas, The Gospel of Truth, The Gospel of Philip,* and *The Gospel of Mary Magdalene,* present Jesus as little more than a teacher of wisdom. The language of wisdom and Gnosticism seem to go hand-in-hand within such a tradition. The publication of *The Other Gospels: Non-Canonical Gospel Texts* (1982) and *The Nag Hammadi Library in English* (1988) have done much to draw some of the best and most probing people to this alternative source of Christian life and thought. The recent popularity of Dan Brown's novel *The Da Vinci Code* (2003) is good evidence of this trend, revealing a spiritual hunger that will consume any sort of paper-thin literature about religion. To be fair, a convergence between the wisdom and mystical traditions of the West and East seems to have real possibilities when the Gnostic texts are held up as the authentic sayings of Jesus, as many have tried to do. But this brings up some important questions: Do the Gnostic texts contain the genuine sayings of Jesus? If so, why are they not in the Christian canon? Why are so many drawn to such secret sayings and sutras while regarding the biblical text as the problem? A study of the Beatitudes offers us a way of hearing and heeding the sayings of Jesus, and, in doing so, placing the Gnostic texts in a better perspective. There are good reasons why the Gnostic texts were not included in the canon. Sitting at the feet of the Beatitudes will reveal what those reasons are by providing us with a more integrated vision of the biblical Jesus in opposition to the more dualistic Jesus of the Gnostics.

The Beatitudes are a treasure trove of wisdom, but the wisdom of the Beatitudes is quite different than the wisdom of the Gnostic tradition. Sadly, the Beatitudes, in all their depth, breadth, and power have been largely ignored, sanitized, and domesticated by the Church. Often,

14

only the more radical clan within the Church has taken the Beatitudes with some seriousness, and they should be offered many a kudo for doing so.

Within the historic life of the Church, many Christians have made a great deal of getting their creeds, dogmas, and confessions right. Much division, schism, and fragmentation has occurred as a result. The split between dogma and wisdom is quite trendy these days. Wisdom is seen as that which unites, confessions as that which divides. Wisdom is seen as that which touches the heart and is transformative. Creeds are good for the rational mind, but they don't deal with our deeper longings and desires. This dualism is understandable, but it is also unhelpful. What we need is a contemplative theology that is grounded in the creeds but is more than mere intellectual assent to such propositions. Our lives should be transformed by the reading of such creeds. If they are not, we must admit to having serious problems. If nothing else, the Beatitudes—one of the central creeds of the Christian faith—are about transformed lives.

We also live in a post 9/11 world. Such an ethos is charged by a passion to combat terrorism and the ensuing clash of civilizations. What do the Beatitudes have to say to a time such as this? Should Christians genuflect to the American empire as the bastion of all that is good in a world dominated by forces of evil and injustice? Surely, the Beatitudes can speak loud and clear to such a situation. The Beatitudes have been called "The Ordination Address to the Twelve," "The Compendium of Christ's Doctrine," "The Magna Charta of the Kingdom," and "The Manifesto of the King." The Beatitudes are the crown jewel of Jesus' ethical vision of the new person, and we can taste the fruit of that ethical vision each time we read them.

The Beatitudes allow us neither the luxury of indulging in the inner journey nor dwelling excessively on the outer journey. They hold the inner and outer journeys in a time-tried and precarious tension. They also knit together the sacred and the profane, spirituality and justice, and the vertical and horizontal dimensions of life. One finds an integrative maturity in the Beatitudes that is not found in the decoy duck of those who make much of spirituality but ignore the demands of justice and peacemaking or those who trample the life of the spirit in the name of justice.

This brief study of the Beatitudes aims to clarify the wisdom of Jesus and explain how his understanding of wisdom and justice has a depth and integrative insight that is lacking in many other forms of spirituality and mysticism. If the Church has tended to domesticate, ignore or sanitize the wisdom teachings of Jesus in the Beatitudes, and the Gnostic tradition—in reaction—has turned to extra-canonical sources in search of the real Jesus, a more radical read of the Beatitudes can offer us a middle way between these two extremes. An integrative and radical read of the Beatitudes will nudge the "one, holy, catholic, and apostolic Church'" to be more responsive to the hard sayings of Jesus. Such a prophetic exegesis also becomes a legitimate questioning of a Gnostic interpretation of Jesus in our post-9/11 context.

Chapter One

Mountain and Valley

Great things are done when men and mountains meet. This is not done by jostling in the street.
William Blake

Seeing the crowds, Jesus went up on the mountain, and when he sat down, his disciples came to him. And he opened his mouth and taught them.
Matthew 5:1–2

The journey from the hurly burly of the valley to the serenity of the mountain, from city to country, town square to desert is a classic mythic structure in most cultures and across the peaks of time. The city and the valley are often seen as places in which the soul is sapped and drained, worn low, and thinned out. The longing for depth, insight, and illumination often begins with a cleansing of the inner life from the toxins and viruses, distractions and diversions of the city. Plato, for example, argued that we are born in a cave, and we often confuse shadows with reality. It is only as we make the journey from the world of shadows in the cave to the blue canopy and clean light of the natural world that we rediscover our true selves.

The pilgrimage, therefore, from valley to mountain is both a literal and a metaphorical journey. The literal hike and trek means leaving behind all the clatter and chatter, all the external demands that take their exacting toll on life and limb. The external silence and quietness that greets those who make such a trip to the high places, deserts, forest dwellings or country settings reveals an inner landscape. The gift of coming to know this inner landscape or inscape is essential to knowing the self at a deeper and more substantive level. Those who do not make such a journey often doom themselves to chasing one illusion after another.

The poet Henrik Ibsen once said, "Take away the life lie of the average person, and you take away their happiness." Henry Thoreau said, "Most men lead lives of quiet desperation." The purpose of the pilgrimage from valley to peak and city to country is to face such life lies and overcome such quiet desperation. The task of taking to the peaks and mountains is, above all else, to separate wheat and chaff, gold and dross from within the soul and spirit. In the stillness and quietness of such places is where each and all must discover deeper resources within.

Contemplative traditions in the West and East, in the Occident and Orient, hold high the need for retreat places in forests, mountains, and desert places. Monasteries are often found in such regions, and many is the saint, guru, fakir, and sage that has been tried and made, shaped and formed on the anvil of peak and desert.

In the Hebrew sacred scriptures, we often find prophets going to the mountains and the wilderness. Moses received the Decalogue on the mountain, and many were the prophets who either lived in the desert or who went there when opposition was most intense. The Jewish people wandered in the desert for forty years before they reached the Promised Land. John the Baptist lived much of his life in the desert, and Jesus often spent time on mountaintops or in the desert. After Jesus, the Qumran community, which preserved the Dead Sea Scrolls, lived in the seemingly barren world of the desert as well.

The contemplative turn to the mountains, country, forest, and desert is a necessary and normal part of the quest for greater inner depth and meaning. In such places—if mind and heart are attentive—a fuller, finer, and more nuanced vocational vision emerges. The Self, in short, is remembered and recovered, the rock hard core of our Being restored. The dirt, smudge, and mud are wiped clean from the inner diamond. Finally, all is seen for what it truly is.

Many can make such trips but never do the demanding work that such an inner hike requires. Taking the literal journey is no guarantee that the inner and metaphorical pilgrimage will be made. The literal journey to such places is a necessary but insufficient condition for substantive transformation. All of us must face the dark places, fears, and insecurities within before real change can occur. If we seek insight, we must go into the caves, look the shadows straight on, ford raging streams, and ascend steep rock trails. When demands become more difficult, the temptation is to give up and turn back. But it is at precisely such crossroads that the differences and distinctions between a dilettante/voyeur and a true pilgrim/saint are revealed.

The process of taking to the peaks, deserts, and forest dwellings speaks little about the content of what is revealed in such places. It is important that means and ends, process and content be discussed. The mere turning to such sites of pilgrimage is part of the answer, but there is much more to be pondered. The spiritual elite in Herman Hesse's *Glass Bead Game* (2002) lived on the peaks of Castalia, but Hesse mocked their limited, immature, and questionable understanding of the spiritual journey. In the same way, Martin Heidegger spent a great deal of time in his cabin in the Black Forest at Todtnauberg, but the lack of content in his notion of Being (*Sein*) and his contemplative philosophy made him susceptible to Nazi thought. Many are the mystics and contemplatives who have wreaked havoc with themselves and others by turning to the peaks, desert, and country and returning not with transformative wisdom but soul-sapping counterfeits.

The turn to such places, therefore, begs a deeper question: Who or what is being met, heard, and received at such inner and outer places? It also illustrates how much we need spiritual maps and probing questions. Those who turn to the peaks can see a variety of things. Suiter's *Poets on the Peaks* makes it quite clear that the content of such a journey can mean different things to different people. Many Westerners turn to the peaks and find only that the content of the East holds them. Some turn to the peaks and never return to the valley and city. Others, like Heidegger, are open to much darkness when they return from their retreats in such places. Hence, the question of content and process, means and end, map and journey must be held in tension.

Matthew tells us that Jesus went up to the mountain. The crowds were demanding their exacting due on both Jesus and the disciples in the valley, and Jesus realized something deeper and more substantive had to be taught to those nearest and dearest to him. The process of turning to the mountain, as we have seen, is a vital and valid requirement of the journey. Jesus, of course, came from a tradition in which the teacher, rabbi, sage or scholar had disciples, and it was the role and responsibility of such an elder or *Abba* to transmit such living wisdom to his followers and disciples.

Sadly, the traditional role of a sage and spiritual father (*Abba*) was and is quite different from that embodied by many university professors and other teachers of higher education today. The latter tends to pass on facts, information, statistics, and technical skills, but rare is the professor that is concerned with insight, wisdom, illumination, and character development. Part of the reason for this, of course, is that intellectual knowledge can be quantified, evaluated, and graded. Character, on the other hand, is about quality, depth, insight, and illumination for the journey, and achievements in these areas are not so easy to assess. Knowledge and information tend to dominate life in the Academy. Hence, many of the most sensitive look elsewhere to slake a deeper thirst. Jesus lived, moved, and had his being within a wisdom tradition. Like most sages, he was much more concerned with inner depth and integrity than with the squirrel-like accumulation of more data. The hike up the hillside to the mountain was about passing on such a vision to the disciples, who would then carry on his mission.

The crowds were left behind in the valley. Much was still and quiet on the rock rim of the mountain. What was the content of such a teaching?

Before beginning to answer such a question, let us turn to the way Matthew prepares us for the wisdom teaching of Jesus. Matthew says, "Seeing the crowds, Jesus went up to the mountain" (Matthew 5:1). It is important to linger here for a few moments.

The Greek word for "seeing" (*eidos*) used in this passage means, "to see the visible form, shape, appearance or outward show." When Jesus looked at the crowds, he was only looking at their outer longings and appearances, their desires for secondary things. He knew something more substantive than miracles and external healings were required to move them from where they were to where he wanted them to be. These were but signs, but many in the crowd confused the signs with the Being to which they pointed, and so they clamored for still more. Jesus knew he had to take his followers to higher places, to walk them to the harder and more demanding truths he had come to tell one and all. The trip up the mountain was the beginning of such a journey.

The Greek word for mountain (*oros*) is the root word from which we get the English words "oracle" and "oracular." The mountains and peaks, in short, were seen in the Classical world as places of insight and illumination. The trip up to such places was done with a purpose. The hope was that by making the journey, a word from the Divine would break through. The high places were seen as closer to God, needful places to be if one hoped to hear God in a clear and direct way.

When Jesus reached the rock rim, he sat down. This action is significant for two reasons: When a sage, rabbi or philosopher sat down in the ancient world, it was a signal to his students that he was about to say something of significance. His change in posture alerted the disciples that they also needed to change their posture to a listening stance if they were to hear him. Second, the root of the Greek word for "to sit" (*katharos*) means "to be pure and clean." This implies that a teacher can only teach effectively when insights are offered from a place of inner integrity. When the Pope speaks *"ex cathedra,"* for example, he speaks from a place in which he has listened deep from a pure heart and mind. The word "cathedral" comes from the same root word. So when Jesus sat, he did so to indicate that he was speaking from a place of inner listening, internal purity, and no crooked lines. The disciples certainly knew they were about to hear something of great import.

Matthew says Jesus opened his mouth and began teaching the disciples. The Greek word used for "open" (*anoia*) can mean, "to create an opening, to rebuild, to build up, to use language in a positive and constructive way to point to more meaningful truths." It can also mean, "to do things in a senseless and foolish way." Language does have this Janus-like quality. It can be used to open up new paths on the journey or used to point the way to cul-de-sacs and rabbit trails. When Jesus opened his mouth to teach, he used the signs and symbols of language to point the way to a new life, a transformed life, a life with meaning and purpose, a life lived within the tension of mountain and valley.

Chapter Two

Home of the Soul

Those who truly hear and practice what I have told you are like a wise person who has built his or her home on a solid rock. The rain falls down, waters rise, and the winds beat against the place, but it stands firm and strong, because its foundation is on the rock. But those who hear what I have taught and do not put such insights into practice are like foolish people who build their home on a sand foundation. The rain will cascade down, the streams will rise, and the winds will blow. Such a home will fall because the foundation is on sand and is weak.

Matthew 7: 24–27

Both Matthew and Luke record the Beatitudes. Matthew's account is more comprehensive than Luke's, but in the main, both men say much the same thing. It is important to note at this point that the content of the Sermon on the Mount and the Beatitudes was probably taught again and again to the disciples and others. In all probability, the Beatitudes were taught in parts and pieces when Jesus thought it was fitting to pass on some word of insight. It is quite possible there were times and seasons when much of the Sermon and the Beatitudes were taught at the same time. The visits up and down the mountains could and would have been retreat times for Jesus and the disciples. These would have been periods of time when he would have sat down with his followers and clarified for them what he was trying to say and do. The busyness of life in the valley would give place to reflection on the peaks about what was learned in the hustle and bustle of life below. It was in these longer periods of silence and stillness that the compact insights of the Beatitudes would have been taught in a fuller manner. It was the task of Matthew and Luke to thread such aphorisms together.

The Beatitudes are like the introduction to the Sermon on the Mount. Jesus concludes the Sermon with the analogy of the soul as a home. We either build our soul on a firm foundation that can withstand the rains, winds, and storms of time, or we build the home of our soul on a foundation of sand. The choice is ours, but there are consequences to be faced either way. It might take time for such consequences to play themselves out, but there is no doubt the whirligig of time will bring to us the costs of decisions made or not made.

The Christian contemplative tradition has often used the home as an analogy for the soul. Not only does the soul have a foundation, it also has many rooms, which we chose to decorate, dwell in or ignore. We are quite eager to have others come in and dine in some of the rooms of the inner life. There are other rooms, however, that we fear to visit, rooms we have locked up and upon whose doors we have placed a "No Trespassing" sign. Much hinges on how we build the foundation of our soul, what parts we leave open, and what parts we close off,.

A healthy home has a strong foundation and is decorated well within and without. Windows are open to the light and warmth of Day Star as well as cleansing winds and breezes that waft across the land. There is no doubt that Jesus longs for us to build the home of our soul on a solid foundation, but he wants us to make them places of comfort and hospitality as well. A home that has many dark and hidden places where secrets are stored away in shadows is not a place of hope and healing. Only as we are willing to visit these dark places, to open doors and rooms that have been long sealed off can the home of the soul become what it is meant to be.

If the inner life can be compared to a house that needs to be built well both within and without, what does such an architectural plan look like, in both theory and practice? This is what the Beatitudes articulate for the sensitive seeker.

Chapter Three

Gifts and the Formation of Character

There are many who might often use the mantra "Lord, Lord," but this is no guarantee they are part of my Kingdom. It is only by living forth my teachings and being true to my Father in heaven that my real disciples are known. In fact, many will say this: "We prophesied, drove out demons, and performed many miracles in your name." Sadly so, I will have to tell many who hold high such gifts, "I do not know you. It is best that you go from me."
Matthew 7:21–23

In religion, too, we must keep a critical attitude that never unconditionally accepts any socially established form of revelation. Otherwise, we are back to idolatry again, this time self-idolatry rather than idolatry of nature, where devotion to God is replaced by the deifying of our present understanding of God.
Northrop Frye, The Double Vision

Right before Jesus took the disciples up the mountain, he and his followers were busy in the valley doing all sorts of healings and miracles. Crowds clustered about in the thousands, either to be healed or to watch the miracle worker in action. It is never difficult to bring large numbers of people together when there is a promise of some sort of spectacular event. People gather like bees round a hive when an event or an individual offers cures for a variety of ills. The past was no different than the present in this regard. Many are eager to visit or follow teachers and healers if they seem to offer instant solutions to the trying problems of the human journey. We have never lacked for sellers of silver bullets and snake oil in the history of religion. Miracle-mongers and groupies are ever in our midst. For many, Jesus had become just such a miracle worker and healer, a "thaumaturgist," and the crowds arrived from many a town and village to see and be helped by such a man.

Although my tone above is somewhat critical, we should never discount or dismiss the importance of healing and miracles. Those who suffer and have suffered with besetting ailments, ongoing pain and one tragedy after another, predictably long for some end or reprieve from their sadness and pain. Who would not want to heal or help a child, man or woman who is suffering from a painful disease? Jesus, to his loving credit, felt the suffering and pain of others and sought to bring temporary ease to such onerous situations.

The rise of the charismatic and renewal movements, with their emphasis on God's healing power, should be welcomed and acknowledged. Much good has been done to and for many people as a result of them. Their life-giving influence has brought much help and assistance to many. This is the positive side to such movements, and Jesus, in his day, was at the forefront of such a cutting edge. Unfortunately, however, such renewal and charismatic movements have their dark side as well.

Three nagging concerns emerge when the healing/miracle journey is embarked upon. First, why is it that many are never healed? In fact, why is it that most who suffer in terrible and tragic ways never find ease from their pain? The notion that all will be healed if just enough prayer is engaged and obvious or hidden sins are ferreted out is just too simple. Such a magical and superstitious approach to suffering and evil does not answer the hard questions of unresolved sicknesses and disease. Second, there is a danger in many renewal movements that gifts and wonder workings come to replace the deeper issues of character development and inner transformation. The means becomes the ends, and the more important ends are eclipsed by the quick fix of magical solutions to more persistent problems. The miracle circuit can easily become like a drug, which is most addictive. Cheap grace becomes a substitute for the hard and demanding work of the inner journey toward wholeness and holiness. Costly grace, unlike cheap grace, is about a lifelong pilgrimage rather than some magical solution that never addresses the deeper issues. The purpose of healing, at its most significant level, is the cure of the soul, and this is a life journey. Third, the marketplace of gifts can also become a battlefield in which renewal leaders compete to outdo and outshine one another. Constant feuds and battles erupt about which gifts are more important and who has these gifts to a greater degree. The chiefs of such sectarian movements often break off from other sects over such clashes. It can all become quite sad and silly.

Jesus was never against doing miracles, casting out demons, giving prophetic utterances or performing healings. But his concern was more about the ends than the means. Healing and miracles cannot solve the deeper issues of human transformation and the need to grow in wisdom and character. It is quite common for healers to gather large crowds, but when the show does not please the crowds, the crowds go elsewhere. Many followed Jesus when he was healing others, but few were around when he went to the cross.

The clash between gifts and character is a perennial one. Immature and shallow religion tends to play up the former while downplaying or censuring the latter. Many use charismatic gifts to indulge and inflate their ego and, in the process, distort the very reason for the gifts. Unlike its counterfeits, serious and mature religion deals with the trying and difficult journey of facing dark places within and working with and through them. Most of the deepest weeds in the human soul take years to root out. Even when such weeds are pulled out, others emerge with a vengeance. Those who ignore the weeds within and overemphasize the gifts distort authentic and genuine religion. This is why Jesus made it clear as he concluded the Sermon that many would cast out demons, heal, and prophesy in his name, but he would not know them (Matthew 7: 21–23), because they would really be doing it for themselves, not him.

At the deepest level, Jesus was more concerned about the state of the inner life and how we can move from bondage to the illusory ego to a place of living from the eternal and reborn Self. This is the real miracle, the journey from a life in chains and shadows, a life colonized and enslaved by the ego, which is the real prison. Jesus came to release people from such bondage, to set them free to be who they were truly meant to be. This process, though, has no instant or magical solution. Many battles must be fought to rediscover and reclaim that which is real and life-giving. Many are the sabotages and deceptions that lead to confusion and emptiness.

The process of cleaning out and living fully within a renovated home of the soul is what Jesus came to teach us. Gifts, miracles, healing, and prophecy are all good. But if not guided, formed, and directed by solid character, they can become an idol, a form of taking God's name in vain. Jesus warns us about this, and we do well to heed his warning. We need prophetic people, healers, and those who work miracles. But even more than this, we need men and women whose character has been forged on the hard anvil of eternity. Such people are made of gold rather than silver, bronze or clay.

Chapter Four

Perfection and Self-Knowledge

Be perfect as your Father in heaven is perfect.
Matthew 5:48

It is rather intimidating to think we are called to be perfect, just as it is baffling to ponder what being perfect means. Is perfection even possible for a mere human? Surely this is asking much too much. Doesn't such a request merely create and produce guilt and unrealistic standards? What did Jesus mean when he said this?

The Greek word for perfect (*telos*) had a long and worthy lineage in the Classical world of Greek and Roman philosophical and theological thought, and Jesus was very much a child of this ethos. What was Jesus getting at when he used this word to point in such a direction? Just as it is natural for a bird to spread its wings and take to the blue canopy, a fish to delight in the waters, an acorn to become an oak, an apple tree to produce apples, and a colt to become a horse, so it is natural for our new nature in Christ to live forth the Beatitudes. All things have a nature (*physis*), and their perfection or proper end is to fulfill their nature. All things have a potential, and within the seed of all things is the ability to actualize such a potential. Given time and the right conditions, a sunflower seed will produce a tall and attractive sunflower plant. This is the nature and perfection of the sunflower seed. It is one thing to suggest that in the natural world, plants and animals fulfill their natures in an involuntary and predictable manner. But what about humans? The main difference is that our perfection is also a matter of the will. Even so, the notion of nature and fulfilling our destiny has some truth to it.

What is human nature in a general sense, and does each person have a unique nature? This is what Jesus and the Classical world taught. We are not an open-ended project, a blank piece of paper or an empty canvas. Our perfection consists in knowing what is deep within us and living out of such a life-giving source. The task of knowing and loving that which is at our core and living from such a place is, in fact, the deepest freedom.

A bird could use its freedom to dive into the water and stay there. It would drown in the process, but the freedom is there. If a bird did this, freedom would trump nature, and life would end. A fish could use its freedom to flip up on the sand, bask in the sun, and never return to the water. Naturally, the fish would die in the process. If a fish did this, freedom would trump nature, and soon the fish would soon be rotting on the shoreline. As these examples illustrate, there are consequences for violating our nature.

Is there such a thing as human nature though? And if so, how do we come to know such a nature in both a general and a particular way? The Beatitudes are about offering shape and form to a general understanding of human nature. Our perfection and destination on the journey consists in coming to know our nature and living from it.

All things in life must have a form and shape from which to focus and direct energy. A fire without a fireplace can wreak havoc in a house. A river that lacks strong and stately banks becomes diffused and thinned out. The Classical West and East realized this. In Hinduism, this form was called dharma and karma. In Taoism, this form was called the Tao. In the Jewish tradition, the Ten Commandments or Decalogue provided form and focus for the human moral journey. In the Greek and Roman world, natural law was the North Star. In the appendix to *The Abolition of Man* (1965), C. S. Lewis wisely ponders these important points of convergence. The Beatitudes presupposes many of these ideas but takes the discussion to a deeper and more particular level.

The Christian tradition often speaks about the differences between general and specific revelation, reason and faith, philosophy and theology. The latter crowns and fulfills the longings and strivings of the former. The Classical tradition in the East and West agreed that there was such a thing as Nature and ends toward which all things aimed and strove. The contemplative traditions of the East and West attempted again and again to bring some concrete reflections on what such a human nature, when disciplined and trained, might look like in a realized and mature form. The Beatitudes are, in essence, a finger pointing to what human nature can and should be in its finest flowering. They depict the home of the soul in all of its splendor, beauty, and grace.

Thus, when Jesus calls us to be perfect like our Father in heaven, he is really saying that just as God is pure Being and true to his nature (and he can be no other), so our perfection consists in being true to the being deep within us that is ever struggling to emerge and live fully. We will never be content until we live from such a place. If we violate our deeper nature, we doom ourselves to a slow death, just as the bird that dove in the water and the fish that flopped onto land. We only begin to live full lives when we seek to conform ourselves to our true nature. This is what it means to be perfect: to know the deepest part of our new nature within, and to live out of that centre.

The difficulty, as I mentioned above, is to know what our nature—our end—truly is. We have forgotten who we are meant to be, and we are often out of touch with what is deeper and more authentic. But if Jesus is God incarnate, and he truly knows our true home and hearth, then it does us well to heed what he has to say about human nature and the work and discipline required to discover and live out of such a place. "Be perfect as your Father in heaven" means, in short, be true to your nature. Cultivate the garden, prune and weed, and bring forth truth, goodness, and beauty. Much hinges on truly knowing and loving what we are called to become. The Beatitudes point out the way for such a journey.

Chapter Five

Blessedness and Deification

God became human so humans could be divinized.
St. Athanasius

The beginning of each Beatitude is often translated as "Blessed are…" or "Happy are those…" While there is some legitimacy to this interpretative approach, such an exegesis actually obscures a fuller vision.

Two words in Greek speak of a full, meaningful, and authentic life. When Aristotle thought of the person who lived a life of excellence, he used the word *eudaimon* to describe them. Those who lived the good life, who attuned themselves to the best and noblest of Classical ideals had attained a higher state of being, and it was thought that they had a more settled experience and understanding of the life journey.

Matthew does not use such a term though when beginning each of the Beatitudes. He uses a more elevated Greek word (*makarios*), which cannot truly be translated as "blessed" or "happy." The root meaning of *makarios* is *makar*, and *makar* means "the inner poise and vision of the gods." In short then, those who internalize and embody the teachings of the Beatitudes in thought, word, and deed will know what it means to live the Divine Life. This shocking notion is at the heart and core of the Christian ethical and ontological vision. Christians are not merely called to live a higher ethical life. They are, in fact, meant to become a different kind of being. The Divine Life is meant to infuse, reshape, reform, and transform Christians so that they will be raised to a new level of existence. In contrast, the highest of the Classical natural virtues is but a false peak or foothill along the way to the highest of all Divine peaks. The Orthodox tradition within Christianity has understood this transition best. They use the language of deification or divinization (*theosis*) to articulate this higher and more supernatural life. Christ has come to point the way and empower those who follow him to walk the way to a Divine Life. This means, therefore, that the Beatitudes are not primarily an ethical system. They are about becoming of the same being, nature, and substance as God. It is impossible to miss this point when we allow the meaning of *makar* and *makarios* to saturate our understanding of the text.

How do we live such a life though? How do we move from the valley, in which we are preoccupied with that which is unimportant, to the higher natural life that we find in the best of Eastern and Western contemplative thought, and then on to the peaks of the supernatural life? What does the map to such places look like, and how do we make the journey to such vistas?

Each of the Beatitudes begins and ends with a peak and positive insight, but there is a valley to be hiked between. There is no resurrection without the cross, no Divine Life without many a death and letting go. The narrow and constrictive skin of the ego must be broken for rich wine to flow through. The Divine Life can only be experienced by letting go of the worst of the unnatural and the best of the natural life. It is this higher, Divine Life that the Beatitudes open us up to consider, to long for and to live.

So far, I have used a variety of analogies to describe the soul. I have compared it to a well renovated and decorated home, a garden that is well tended; a fire that is in need of a safe place to burn, and a river in need of stable and stately banks. All things have a nature and an end. The soul is no different. But how do we recognize the Divine Life of the soul, and how is such a life to be lived?

We know, for example, what doctors, pilots, teachers, carpenters, farmers, conductors, electricians, builders, artists, and dentists are meant to be and do, and we evaluate them according to how well they conform to their training. If they violate our expectations, we can bring them to the dock. If we can make sense of the nature of such vocations and skills, and we can know the difference between counterfeits and the real thing within such trades (because there are strict standards and a plumb line), how can we recognize those who are being trained to live the Divine Life? Many can say they are Christians, committed to a spiritual search, just as anyone can say they are a doctor, dentist, carpenter, pilot, nurse or architect. Of course, the mere saying of something does not make it so. There are criteria by which we can know the difference between good, better, best, and bad, worse, and worst in terms of people's vocations. If so, the same must be true when it comes to evaluating where we are at on our spiritual journey. Fair enough, but what criteria should we use?

The answer, once again, can be found in the Beatitudes. They are a solid, sensible, and sane criterion for evaluating where we are at on the path to the Divine Life and when we have settled for a lesser and more limited understanding of it. The last few pages have circled hawk-like over the terrain and background of the Beatitudes. Now it is now time to allow such sayings to speak directly to us.

Chapter Six

Ego Dies, Self Is Born

The Divine Life is for those who die to the demands of the ego.
Such people will inhabit the Kingdom of Heaven.
Matthew 5:3

From wrong to wrong the exasperated spirit
Proceeds, unless restored by that refining fire
Where you must move in measure, like a dancer
T. S. Eliot, *Four Quartets* (Little Gidding)

The human condition is one of being pulled in different directions. Plato compared this to a chariot driver who has a white and dark horse by the reins. The dark horse pulls the chariot toward a cliff's edge and inevitable destruction. The white horse pulls the chariot toward splendid peaks that overlook evocative vistas of beauty. Plato also compared the soul to a ship with many sailors. Each sailor on the ship thinks he knows best how to guide the ship across the waters. The sailors, like many conflicting desires, can capsize the craft or lead to a mutiny. If the ship lacks a good captain, it can veer in all sorts of directions. The human condition is about either allowing a good and wise captain to order our desires or being victimized by an evil and unwise captain.

Our many desires, though, are merely symptoms of something much deeper at work in the depths of our being. There is, in fact, a war going on between the ego (the dark horse) and the self (the white horse). How do we know the difference between the ego and the self, and, more importantly, how can we allow the white horse to lead us across the plains and hillocks of time while keeping the black horse properly reined in? Such decisions need much discernment. In *New Seeds of Contemplation* (1961), Thomas Merton spoke clearly on this issue:

> *Contemplation is precisely the awareness that this 'I' is really 'not I,' and the awakening of the unknown 'I' that is beyond observation and reflection and is incapable of commenting upon itself. Our external, superficial ego is not spiritual. Far from it, the ego is doomed to disappear as completely as smoke from a chimney. It is utterly frail and evanescent.*[1]

Jesus often compared the soul to a seed that must die in the soil before the self can be born. St. Paul also made the distinction between the "Old Adam" and the "New Adam." At the heart of the Christian notion of the Incarnation is the compelling fact that God, in Christ, emptied himself (*kenosis*) so he could be one with us. There is no eternal life without letting go, emptying, bidding *adieu* to the dark horse, the ego, and the chains that so often shackle us.

Echoing Jesus' teaching, German mystic Meister Eckhart said, "The shell must be cracked apart if what is in it is to come out for if you want the kernel you must break the shell." St. Augustine spoke often about the inevitable tension and clash between *caritas* and *cupiditas*, between the desire to live on the level of passionate love and the desire to indulge and pander to the ego. St. John of the Cross spoke of the important difference between facing the *nada* (or nothingness of the ego) and stepping into the dark night of the soul where all finite things (including the ego) dissolve and dissipate before the light of the Divine. In time, such a journey will open a person to the fullness (*todo*) of the self, which is the image and likeness of God.

In *Zen Flesh, Zen Bones* (1994), Paul Reps tells a graphic and never to be forgotten tale: Nan-In, a Zen master, had a university professor visit him. Nan-In served the professor tea in the best of the tea ceremony traditions. The master kept filling the clean cup until the hot tea spilled over the rim and onto the professor's lap. Finally, the startled professor could contain himself no longer. "Can't you see that is tea is spilling all over me?" He cried out. Nan-In stopped poring the tea. Then he said, "You are like this cup. You are so full of your opinions, facts and information. How can I show you Zen unless you first empty the cup of your ego?"[2] As this story illustrates, the cup of your soul can be filled with ego or self. Much hinges on what you allow in and what you allow to stay in the cup of your soul.

Canadian literary critic Northrop Frye placed the dilemma and vision of the Christian good news in illuminating context in *The Double Vision: Language and Meaning in Religion* (1991) when he said:

> *Inside one's natural and social origin, however, is the embryo of a genuine individual struggling to be born. But this unborn individual is so different from the natural man that Paul has to call it by a different name. The New Testament sees the genuine human being as emerging from an embryonic state within nature and society into the fully human world of the individual, which is symbolized as a rebirth or second birth, in the phrase that Jesus used to Nicodemus. Naturally this rebirth cannot mean any separation from one's natural and social context, except insofar as a greater maturity includes some knowledge of the conditioning that was formerly accepted uncritically. The genuine human thus born is the soma pneumatikon, the spiritual body (1 Corinthians 15:44). This phrase means that spiritual man is a body: the natural man or soma psychikon merely has one. The resurrection of the spiritual body is the completion of the kind of life the New Testament is talking about, and to the extent that any society contains spiritual people, to that extent it is a mature rather than a primitive society.[3]*

This Beatitude walks us to the toughest and most demanding depths of our being. The Classical world tended to see humans in a tripartite manner. There was the body or material aspect of being human (*sarx* and *soma*), the intermediate and mediating part of being (*psyche*), and—in the deepest part of us—our spirit (*pneuma*). The Classical tradition taught that these three parts of our being were integrated and connected. Each part could and would have an impact on the other. Body, soul, and spirit each had the potential for good and nobility as well as evil and mediocrity. It was not, as some falsely assume and as some Gnostics thought, that spirit was good and the body subordinate. If we are ever to be transformed from the depths of the inner life out, it is imperative that such a change begins at the level of the spirit and then continues outwards to the body. This is why, in the Greek, the first Beatitude suggests we must be absolutely destitute in the area of the spirit (*pneuma*). This takes us to the foundation level of transformation and change where the real renovation of the soul begins. Until we are willing to die on a spiritual level, our so-called spirituality can be as egotistic and narcissistic as our soul or body. This Beatitude takes us beyond such a simplistic dualism into a much more profound understanding of spiritual rebirth. Death must occur on all levels so that the new person will emerge at all levels. Merton described this process well in his classic tract for the times, *The New Man* (1961).

The first Beatitude, therefore, asks us to let go of the fiction of the ego (with all of its diversions and distractions). We are asked to empty the cup of the body, soul, and spirit; because only as such a cup is empty can it be filled with the clean water of the Eternal.

The first Beatitude has often been translated as "Blessed are the poor of spirit, for the kingdom of heaven is for them." It is important to note that there are two words in Greek for poor (*penes* and *ptochos*). *Penes* means, "a person who is not destitute but does not have much," whereas the poverty of *ptoches* means, "absolute poverty." Jesus is saying that until we reach the point in which we see the absolute poverty and destitution of the ego, we have yet to begin the real journey. Only as we allow ourselves to be emptied can we be filled with a more substantive life.

As I noted earlier, each Beatitude begins and ends with a peak promise, but between each peak is a dark and difficult valley through which we must pass. We are promised the Divine Life if and when we let go of the ego, allow the seed to die, empty the cup, bid *adieu* to the

Old Adam, leave the cave of shadows, and throw off the shackles and chains that bind us. This is what, at the deepest level, Christian liberty is all about. No more can we be colonized and enslaved by the shallow and unsubstantial. Our deeper self longs to break through the chrysalis and live. We are finally free to fly as we were originally meant to. This is the promise of the first peak.

The second peak is about dwelling in the Kingdom of Heaven. What does this mean? We must be careful not to over-spiritualize the notion of the Kingdom of Heaven. Sadly, both the Church and Gnostics often do exactly that. Let us not forget though that Jesus was a Jew, and for a Jew, the Kingdom was about a material and political reality. It was about the inner life, but it is also about the outer world of justice and peace. There is no way that the Kingdom of Heaven (*Basileia ton ouranon*) can be reduced to merely an internal reality. This means that those who let go of the ego and rein in the dark horse enter a community that is as concerned with the inner journey as the outer journey. The Kingdom of Heaven, like Eternal Life, is not something that is postponed for the life after this one. It is virtually impossible to get such an interpretation from the text. The Kingdom of Heaven is about a quality of existence lived and experienced in time but fulfilled and consummated at the end of time. The first fruits are tasted here. The feast is at trail's end.

In summary, the first Beatitude promises us a taste of the Divine Life if and when we are willing to let go and die to the ego. The journey through many a dark night and darker cave points to other white-capped peaks on the far side of the valley. We are offered the opportunity to live in a kingdom that is infused with justice and peace. This Beatitude is not about spiritual individualism and a private journey. Mature spirituality is both communal and political, and this is where Jesus is pointing. Such a communal and political journey is lived in time and history while look-ing beyond both. If the Divine Life and God's Kingdom are promised us if we turn our backs on the toxic nature of the ego, what does this Divine and Kingdom Life look like in more depth and detail? If we are called to empty the cup of the ego and banish the thieves in the home of the soul, with what will the cup be filled, and how will our homes be renovated and decorated? This points us to the second Beatitude.

(Footnotes)

[1] Thomas Merton. *New Seeds of Contemplation.* New York: New Directions, 1961, pp. 7–8.

[2] Paul Reps. *Zen Flesh, Zen Bones.* Boston: Shambhala Publications, 1994, p. 5.

[3] Northrop Frye. *The Double Vision: Language and Meaning In Religion.* Toronto: University of Toronto Press, 1991, pp.13–14.

Chapter Seven

Suffering and Hope

The Divine Life is for those who have lived through tragedy and suffering. Such people will be comforted at a deep level.
Matthew 5:4

I do not ask the bleeding how he feels. I become the bleeding man.
Walt Whitman

There are those who skim over the waters of time and seem not to notice or seriously internalize the suffering of many or the tragic side of life. Such Pollyanna types purchase their sunny disposition by ignoring much sadness and evil in this world. Eat, drink, and be merry becomes the motto for such untried optimists, and their lives are paper-thin as a result. In contrast are those who dive deep beneath the water. The deeper they plunge, the more they see of the dark and hard things of life. Such pessimistic and depressive types are acutely aware of the negative side of life, but, like Hamlet, they become paralyzed by what they see and hear. The former is quick to act but the action is often shallow and thin. The latter is slow to act, but the action taken is often more substantive.

The first Beatitude urges us to let go of the ego, to empty the cup so we can be filled by something more substantive. The second Beatitude guides us into how the inside of the cup or the interior of the home should be filled or decorated. We can always know when we are in the presence of those who are near to God if they are sensitive to human suffering and human struggles. The most sensitive people feel the hurt and pain of the world, and they refuse to walk away from such persistent sadness. But those who have antennae for both external and internal pain can also become overwhelmed by that very same gift.

The peaks of the second Beatitude are the Divine Life offered and much comfort given through such clouds of unknowing. The valley cuts deep, and the dark places through which one must pass can destroy the soul. The difficult task is to live forth from the depths of pain and suffering while holding on to hope. It is on the Divine anvil that such a vision is made and formed.

The second Beatitude makes it clear that as we open ourselves to the Divine Life, we will experience God's compassionate and suffering love for the world. We will also know God's comfort and peace in the midst of such struggles. The Greek word for comfort in this Beatitude is *parakleitos*. This word is often used for the Spirit of God. It is important to note that *klesis* and *kletos* mean, "called, invited or summoned by God." Those who are called by God will be open to the suffering of the world, but they will not be overwhelmed by it. Such people will know, in the depths of their lives, the comfort, stillness, grace, and kindness of God.

The second Beatitude clearly points the way to a life of faith that is about neither a silly optimism nor a trivial triumphalism. The Christian life is about costly rather than cheap grace. A theology of glory must walk hand-in-hand with a theology of the cross. There is no eluding this inevitable tension. The Divine Life can only be known to the degree we are at one with others in their suffering, but there is more to the journey than merely sitting in suffering. There is also hope and comfort. But such gifts are offered only to those who care enough to sit, often silently, with others in their pain. The home of our soul should be a place for others to come and rest, to be still and comforted. If the home of our soul is not this, then we need to question the sort of home we have built and what is in inside of it.

The reality of the human condition and the tragic nature that characterizes much of it raises some important questions. Do we only sit with those who suffer? How should we respond to the tragedies and evils of life? What stirs within us when we see and feel such things? This points the way to the third Beatitude.

Chapter Eight

Passion and the Quest for the Good

The Divine Life is for those who bring their passions under control
for goodness. It is such people that will inherit the earth.
Matthew 5:5

The third Beatitude builds carefully and thoughtfully on the earlier Beatitudes. The home of the soul is to be emptied of clutter and litter, dust and debris. Thieves that have broken in and wrecked havoc with the place are to be thrown out. The owners of the place are meant to make it a place of beauty and hospitality. Those who are most welcome are those who have suffered the deepest and most intense pain and seen some of the worst tragedies on the human journey. Sitting with such people arouses a sense of anger at the scarred bodies and bruised souls. But such a renovated home is actually meant to be a place of healing for such pain and a place for new memories to emerge.

This Beatitude has often been translated as "Blessed are the meek/humble, for they will inherit the earth." We need to stop and ponder this translation, and what it has often meant for many. In the English language, meekness and humility have often been equated with being rather spineless, a doormat. The Greek word for "meek" (*praus*) has two meanings. Plato and Aristotle used this word as an important ethical pointer. It meant a middle way between extremes. The cardinal and theological virtues in the Classical tradition were viewed as a middle path or *via media* between the extremes of the vices. This was the first meaning of *praus*. Such an ordering and disciplining of desires and longings meant an inner watchfulness was required. All humans feel strongly about different things, and it is such passions and commitments that make the human journey what it is. But passions, like red-hot flicking flames of a fire, can create much heat but little light. If passions are not properly ordered and directed, much hurt can come to one and all. This Beatitude does not deny the importance of strong feelings and commitments. In fact, it is better to feel strongly about something than to be inert, passive, and never interested in much. There is something tragic about those who have buried, suppressed, and submerged their passions to the point where they are little more than the walking dead. The third Beatitude calls forth the passions but directs such intense feelings down a certain path.

The second meaning of *praus* was drawn from the world of wild and untamed horses. Many were the high-spirited horses in the ancient world, and most of them roamed free on the hills and uplands. Such creatures were hard to capture and harder still to tame and domesticate. The freedom of the mountains coursed through their majestic bodies. The intensity and passion of such wild creatures was something to be admired and honored. The task was to know how to capture and train the wild horse without dampening its freedom-loving spirit. A good trainer would earn the trust of these upland creatures, train them so a child could eat from their hand, and yet never break their intense spirit and love of the fresh breeze and wind, of the rocks and crags, uplands and mountains. Both meanings of *praus* suggest a similar sense. Feel strongly about life. Be passionate about the human journey. Be like the majestic and wild horses that roamed in the highlands. Do not allow such leanings to be domesticated and sanitized. But put such tendencies in the service of a higher good. This is the tension, of course.

Let me return to the metaphor of the home of the soul. Empty the place of all that is unnecessary. Create a home that welcomes those who have suffered and struggled much. The passions that emerge when hearing such sad tales should arouse feelings of anger and frustration within. The task is to know how to discipline and direct such emotions in the right direction. If this is not done, anger and bitterness can fester, and toxins can pollute the inner life. When this occurs in the inner life, more work is in the offing.

The peaks in the third Beatitude are the promise of abiding in the Divine Life and inheriting the earth. The valley is about doing the hard work of disciplining and ordering passions in a healthy and life-giving direction. It is significant to note that the word "inherit" in this Beatitude is the same root word as in the second Beatitude. *Klesis* and *kletos* win the day yet again. The inherited comfort that comes to those who suffer with the sufferers is fleshed out in more detail in this Beatitude. Those who have entered into the pain and suffering of others, and those who have properly educated and ordered their desires and passions, these are the ones who will inherit the earth. We see here once again that the promise is not some unduly spiritualized notion of faith. The earth, the soil, the land—this is what those who live a life of integrity receive. This is the upland peak on the far side of disciplining the desires. Just as the Kingdom of Heaven (to be understood in a political sense) is given to those who bid *adieu* to their ego, and just as comfort is offered to those who suffer with others, the firm and solid soil is there for those who have been transformed internally. There is the smell of the soil, the body, and the earth in all of this. This is no Gnostic turn to the spiritual realm as a flight from matter and flesh, air and ether, wind and rock rim. Instead, the Beatitudes point the way to a highly integrated and holistic notion of the new life in Christ. There are linguistic connections between healthy, whole, and holy. This more mature and integrated notion of holiness brings together sky and earth, body and spirit, kingdom and home. There is something profoundly ecological and environmental about this Beatitude. But, unlike more romantic, sentimental, and liberal views of the environment, the perspective of the Beatitudes makes clear that the renewal of the earth must include renewal of the human soul as well.

If desires and longings, passions and feelings need to be disciplined and ordered, how is this to take place, and in what direction are they to be pointed? This is the essence of the fourth Beatitude. We have seen quite clearly that the first three Beatitudes thread together in an exquisite way the inner and the outer journey, spirituality and politics, inscape and landscape. This is no different in the fourth Beatitude.

Chapter Nine

Hunger and Justice

The Divine Life is for those who hunger and thirst for justice.
Such people will be fed to the full.
Matthew 5:6

But the fact remains that objective moral standards exist, whether
people know them or not. Choices are made and judged in the
light of objective moral laws, and violation of these laws brings
disaster.
Thomas Merton, *Peace in the Post-Christian Era*

We all hunger and thirst, and our natural hunger and thirst often enslaves us. It also overrides a deeper hunger, a hunger for community in which justice and peace prevail rather than competition and narcissism.

Unfortunately, we have often translated the fourth Beatitude as "Blessed are those who hunger and thirst for righteousness" and then reduced the meaning of "righteousness" to personal and private piety. The text will not grant us this sort of indulgence (no more than the prophets of old). In this Beatitude, Jesus is calling us to be seekers of justice, of the common good, of that which is just for all of us. When the deeper vision of this Beatitude is reduced to a merely private and personal way to live a life of holiness and integrity, we sanitize the text and mute its power and fullness. An interest in spirituality that lacks a hunger and thirst for justice is merely an opiate, a diversion. Justice is

51

about asking why poverty exists, why we war continually, why injustice so often wins the day, who are the power elite that perpetuate such evils, and what can be done about it all. There is, in fact, a moral plumb line by which empires, nations, communities, and individuals can be measured. If we lose this high moral standard that cannot be taken captive by the culture wars of our time, the religious journey can slip into the politics of the right, left, centre or, worse yet, sentimentality or apathy.

It is fascinating to realize that the Greek word for "thirst" (*dipsochos*) can mean, "double-minded, two souls, wavering or two selves." This understanding of "to thirst" is fitting. Our thirsts, desires, and longings can divide us. The more we are internally divided and fragmented, the more we waver and are double-minded. How do we move from having dispersed and fragmented thirsts (for many conflicting things) to thirsting and hungering for the essential, substantive, and important things? This is where the Beatitudes speak clear and clean. We all waver and are double-minded in our thirst. But in the end, what will truly slake it? The longing for justice and goodness. Such an orienting of our thirsts directs our longings and desires to the life-giving rather than life-dividing places. Narrow, indeed, is the gate that takes us to life, and justice is a narrow door that opens up to life abundant.

The Greek word for "justice" (*diakaios*) used in this Beatitude is the same word Plato used in the *Republic*. It was the common term used in the Classical world for the political, economic, and social good. The language of the Kingdom of Heaven and inheriting the Earth now works its way into the fourth Beatitude. The most mature thinkers in the Classical world never separated spirituality and wisdom or being and contemplation from justice (*agathos*) and the good (*hagios*). The Pre-Socratics indulged in a form of theology and philosophy that ignored the world of ethics and politics, but Socrates, Plato, Aristotle, and the Jewish prophets never hiked this simplistic path. Jesus was very much a child of both the Classical world and the Jewish prophetic tradition, and the Beatitudes sum up the Jewish prophetic way in a succinct and compact manner. Therefore, it would be unthinkable for Jesus to elevate wisdom and contemplation and subordinate justice and the good. For Jesus, the criterion of a wise and contemplative life is the depth to which a person lives a good and just existence. Again, such a word (justice) was not merely a personal and private term. Justice and the good were charged with political relevance.

The culture wars that so beset us these days often make it difficult to discern what it means to be just. The political right insists that justice is about traditional family values, pro-life, law and order, retributive justice, large prisons, military expansionism, the death penalty, opposition to gay rights, a market economy, and a commitment by the USA and England to battle terrorism in the world. The political left holds high such hot button issues as pro-choice, pro-gay, alternate family values, a higher role for the state and taxation for the distribution of wealth and support of public education and health care, a serious questioning of aggressive military action, and an eagerness to support rehabilitative and restorative approaches to crime and punishment. Who is right and who is wrong on these ethical issues? What is the just position to take? Is it possible that the political, social, and economic right is insightful in some areas but blind in others? Is it also possible that the political, social and economic left is incisive in some areas but weak of sight in other areas? Is there a more consistent vision of justice that transcends the tribalism of the left, right, and sensible centre? If an ethical vision of justice is ever to be articulated seriously and lived forth, it is imperative that people of faith transcend the ethical and ideological clans that so dominate the public discourse these days. Unless this is done, the language of justice will be co-opted by reactionary conservatism or trendy liberalism. Neither position is capable of pointing the way to a more consistent notion of justice. It is the role of a prophetic stance to move in this direction.

Therefore, the two peaks in this Beatitude deal with orienting our desires and longings toward a hunger for justice and a thirst for the good. Such a turn challenges a form of spirituality that turns its back on the political. Those who live the deified life in God must be agents of justice. This will take such people back into the valley and city from peaks, forests, country, and desert. The hunger and thirst for justice can be frustrating, exasperating, and irritating much of the time. The opposition will be strong, persistent, and never ending. There is a tendency to grow weary, to grow faint and ease up. Lesser thirsts and hungers dominate the day, because they are easier to satisfy. Often, after spending a few years in the thick of the fray, there is a tendency to settle for less and less, to turn to that which numbs the deeper hunger for justice and goodness. Over the long haul, a life lived in the city seeking justice can be spiritually draining and physically and mentally exhausting.

The peak on the far side of this valley is thick with feasting and plenty, but such a bounty is only for those who have hiked the hard trail. The Greek word for "to feed or supply" (*chortazo*) means "to supply in lavish abundance." Those who allow their hunger and thirst to be directed to the highest things will be offered a well spread table. It is also interesting to note that the root word for *chortazo* is *chor*, and the Greek word for dancing is *choros*. Those who truly hunger and thirst for justice and the good will not only be fed at the Divine table, they will also come to know and participate in the eternal round dance. Needless to say, much good can come from such a communal and choreographed life.

It is one thing to hold high the centrality of justice and goodness as essential to the mature and authentic religious life. It is quite another thing to discern the best means by which justice can be embodied. Some who read the Beatitudes interpret them in an idealistic manner, insisting that the only way Divine justice is reflected in an imperfect world is through intentional resistance communities, protest, and anarchist politics. Others argue that advocacy groups are a better way to live forth a just vision in time. Still others suggest that the work of non-government organizations (NGOs) and inter-governmental organizations (IGOs), such as the United Nations, are better still. Many who are well trained in political theory and political science insist that the State (imperfect though it is) and formal political parities are the finest way of ensuring a just and good world in a minimal yet meaningful manner. It is one thing, therefore, to elevate the importance of justice. It is quite another thing, in a practical and prudential way, to ponder how justice, in thought, word, and deed, can be realized and embodied within and between states.

The desire to think through and live forth a just life can be tiring, and the passion for justice can make a person hard. Powerful people and systems will thwart such desires world without end. The task of beating hands and fists against the brick walls of injustice year after year can create deep cynicism and anger. There are many brittle ideologues that hunger for justice and peace, but the hunger can turn rancid and toxic if you are not careful. Some of the best idealists, in time, become angry and bitter cynics. Such people feel they have not been heard, that they are continually on the margins, and that change never comes anyway. Why bother holding high the banner of justice? It is more important to be realistic. This is the wisest way to get through life, they say. The poor will always be with us, so why bother fighting for such people? Thus, the fifth Beatitude comes as a fit walking companion to the fourth, because it illustrates how mercy and justice must walk side-by-side.

Chapter Ten

Mercy and Justice

The Divine Life is offered to those who are gracious and merciful.
Such people will be treated in a merciful and gracious manner.
Matthew 5:7

Those who have a passion for justice and a commitment to goodness are often keen to ask questions about structures and power elites that subvert or minimize the possibility of achieving some sort of imperfect justice. Needless to say, there are various theories and debates about what constitutes justice and how such a definition is to be fleshed out in the real world of politics. Those who have lived in this ethos become only too well aware of how the political right, the sensible centre, and the left (and debates and divisions within each of these tribes) fragment and hike different paths over definitions and ideological commitments.

The longing for justice can, if care and sensitivity is not taken, slip into unkind and bitter warfare, Those who were once friends cease to talk to one another, and those who see the world in different ways can be quite brutal to one another. People often get lost in the ideological shuffle, ideas trump relationships, and much verbal and actual violence can occur. Basic human virtues such as kindness, graciousness, and mercy are often ignored when the battle for justice dominates the stage.

In the midst of this inevitable clash between justice and mercy, the wise insights of Jesus bring clarity and peace once again. When the longing for justice banishes mercy, a brittle and tragic ideology dominates the stage. When mercy and compassion ignore the hard call for justice, sentimentality can win the political day. Only by living of the tension between justice and mercy can a wise, sane, and sensible religious vision come into being. Jesus knew the passion of the political and nationalist Zealots in his day, and he saw where and why violence wormed its way into such a nationalist vision. Jesus was drawn to the passion, but he had problems with the aggressiveness and violence of the Zealots. Jesus neither denied nor ignored the fact that he had come to create a new Kingdom, but his Kingdom is as much about mercy and compassion as it is about justice and goodness. Unfortunately, it is often much easier to divorce mercy and justice than it is to wed them and have them live a long and healthy marriage together. However, the Divine Life is about holding mercy and justice together in a delicate and nuanced way. This is a spiritual discipline in and of itself. Internalizing and living forth the tensions within the Beatitudes is the very essence of a genuine spiritual disciple. All else merely points to this white-hot core.

Chapter Eleven

Catharsis and a Clean Home

The Divine Life is offered to those whose Home is clean on the Inside. Such people will know the very presence of God and see His Face.

Matthew 5:8

It is significant that the sixth Beatitude comes at this place in the journey. The fourth and fifth Beatitudes are about entering the social and political world and attempting to be agents of justice, goodness, mercy, and compassion. The world of politics can be unkind to those who battle for justice in a merciful and gracious way. Unkind things will be said and done, and rejection and indifference are often the order of the day. How are we to respond when we are treated indifferently, when we are marginalized or when untrue things are said about us before others? The predictable danger, of course, is the "fight or flight" syndrome. We can withdraw from the fray, retreating turtle-like under our shells or come out with both guns blazing. Are these the only two options though?

The sixth Beatitude takes us back into the home of the soul for a checkup, a spring cleaning. We have met the Greek word for clean (*katharos*) before. The Beatitudes opens with the same word. The Greek word that Matthew used to describe Jesus sitting, after he ascended the mountain, means to be clean and pure inside. Those who speak from the deepest places must be clean within. If they are not, pollutants are mixed in with the motives and content of their speech.

It is inevitable that many hard things come our way in the midst of the hurly burly of life. We can grow bitter, angry, vindictive, and hardened to others. If and when we do this, we begin to lose ourselves. We forget who we are meant to be. When we keep the home of our soul clean, polished, and well dusted, it becomes a home well worth living in. This means we are in constant need of spring cleanings. Rooms can become musty, dark, and dank. Smells can emerge from hidden and secret places. It is only as we allow ourselves to deal with the many hurts and disappointments in life that we come to know the Divine Life. But this Beatitude promises us even more.

We all see life through a unique set of eyes or windows. The cleaner these eyes or windows are, the more and better we see. But when cataracts grow on the eyes, sight is dimmed. And when a window is smudged or dirty, it muddies the vision. This is as true in the physical world as it is in the spiritual realm. When darkness enters the soul, spiritual sight is minimized. When light returns to the soul, more is seen. Those who have closed the shutters or muddied the windows of their soul will not see Day Star, the blue canopy above or feel the healing balm of the soft wind and inviting breezes. In contrast, those who have opened the windows and shutters of their souls will be flooded with light and warmth.

We can only live the Divine Life and truly see God if and when we are clean. This is not an easy task, and we must work with God to accomplish this goal. The Beatitudes do not allow us to slip into a theology of extreme grace (Augustine/Luther/Calvin) or extreme works (Pelagius/Arminius). The Greek word used here is *synergism*. The combination of God's inviting and generous grace must always be matched by our effort to return to our real nature. We are responsible, with God, for rediscovering and cleaning up the home of our being. This takes much work and effort. Nothing happens instantly or by magic. Our home will only become what it is meant to be if and when we are willing to do the required renovations. Working together with God and within the life of the one holy, catholic, and apostolic Church, we will see clean and clear again. Only through this better way seeing will we finally see God.

But we will never see God if our eyes are covered with cataracts or the windows of our soul are thick with dirt, mud, and sludge.

The peaks in this Beatitude are most inviting, and the scenery exquisite, but much work is needed to ascend to the rock rims where much can be seen for hundreds of snow-capped miles. If we long to be on the roof of the world, only hard hiking will take us there. This is what the Beatitudes tell us. There is no alternate or secret route to such vistas.

In this Beatitude, Jesus walks us back into the interior life. Life in the valley can drain, deplete, deflect, and poison the soul. Therefore, it is essential that the interior castle be kept clean if the exterior journey is going to be substantive and significant. The seventh Beatitude leads us back to the external and social world again. Shuttling to and fro between peak and valley, interior and exterior, and spirituality and justice is the unavoidable tension of the authentic religious journey.

Chapter Twelve

Peacemaking and Justice

The Divine Life is offered to those who are Makers and Creators of Peace. Such people will be called the children of God.
Matthew 5:9

Peace is not the absence of tension. It is the presence of justice.
Martin Luther King, Jr.

Peace has been understood in a multitude of ways. Some assume it means a retreat from the fray, a refusal to enter the hard issues of life. Others see it as a commitment to pacifism. The quest for peace is often set in opposition to war, hence the peacemakers and pacifists are seen as doves, and the warmongers and military men as the hawks. Those who are for peace are opposed to war, so peace equals, from this perspective, some form of active but non-violent protest or intervention. Are there other ways to approach the notion of peace, though, other than the standard and establishment positions? More to the point, what is Jesus trying to say to us about peace in this passage?

To answer this question, we must set the seventh Beatitude within the context of the other Beatitudes. Peace has something to do with inner peace, and such interior peace has a great deal to do with the ordering and educating of desires and longings. A person cannot, in a serious way, be engaged in the larger questions of war and peace if there is no peace within. Many have a passion for peace on a local, national, and global scale, but it is a fragile thing. The interior life of such people is often in shambles, and their involvement in questions of how to peacefully resolve military conflicts becomes anything but peaceful. This is why Jesus makes it clear again and again in the Beatitudes that the inner life must be clean and clear. There should be no crooked lines.

At times, there is a tendency to separate peace and justice. Many see and interpret the meaning of peace in such a way that they never need deal with hard political questions of poverty and systemic injustice. The issue of peace and war is their only concern. All other issues are subordinate to the military one. The attempt to link and integrate justice and peace does raise all sorts of troubling questions and tensions, but living with many tensions is at the heart of the Beatitudes. Peace is not the absence of tension, it is knowing how to live with many tensions in a settled, serene, and centred manner.

The Greek word used here for "peacemaker" can be compared to an artist or poet who paints or writes something life-giving. The artist can bring vision and insight in the midst of a troubling situation. A mature peacemaker, unlike an ideological maker of peace, has the ability to elude and question many stubborn notions of peace that are more tribal than they are thick with wisdom and insight. A peacemaker is a bridge-builder who seeks to bring opposing clans together. However, as any mediator knows, those who do such things are often fired at by both sides. But such is the fate of those who attempt, as Divine artists, to paint something new on the canvas of time.

The long awaited publication of Thomas Merton's *Peace in the Post-Christian Era* (2004) walks the extra mile to raise all of the hard questions (in an internal and external way) about a mature understanding of peacemaking. *Peace in the Post-Christian Era* grounds the discussion in the history of Christian peacemaking, explores options and objections to such a tradition, and offers many solid and sane insights on contemporary questions of war and peace. The "just war" tradition is also discussed, as is its use and abuse. *Peace in the Post-Christian Era* has been called a truly prophetic book, and there is little doubt that it is. The journey into a deeper understanding of peace as articulated by Merton is true to the Beatitudes for the simple reason that the Beatitudes point the way to a prophetic way of understanding the faith journey.

Thomas Merton was, in many significant ways, the 20th century equivalent of Erasmus just as Erasmus was the 16th century embodiment of Merton. Both were prolific writers, both engaged the hot button issues of the time, and both men thought through their peace position from within the Beatitudes. They were soul friends across the white-capped peaks of time, and if we ever hope to have a feel for the rich texture of the Christian view of peacemaking, Erasmus and Merton must be read and internalized. We do not need to read too far into Erasmus's *Enchiridion militis christiani, The Praise of Folly, Adages* or *Colloquies* to get a sense of his thoughtful passion for peace. But, it is in the *Querela Pacis* or *The Complaint of Peace (Peace Protests)* that we enter the fullness and depth of Erasmus's commitment to the Christian vision of peace as interpreted from the Beatitudes and applied to the warlike ethos of the 16th century. Merton did much the same thing in *Peace in the Post-Christian Era*. Both Erasmus and Merton are true teachers, mentors, and *Abbas* within an authentic Christian peacemaking tradition. Neither can be ignored by anyone interested in a demanding approach to making peace.

Both Erasmus and Merton thought and spoke a Christian vision of peace and peacemaking in their era. What does such a peacemaking perspective look like in our post 9/11 world? What does it mean to be peacemakers in a time when those in power have created much fear, when terrorism is seen as a predominant domestic and foreign policy question, and when Anglo-American militarism is unquestioned by many? It does not take a great deal of reflection to realize that 9/11 occurred for real reasons. But how does a State respond to such terrorist acts in a just and peaceful manner (without the State becoming a terrorist itself)? What has been the nature of American foreign policy in the Middle East, and how has such a foreign policy (directly and covertly) created the conditions and climate for terrorists? These sorts of questions must be asked. If they are not, a reactionary and hawkish mentality comes to sit on the throne. This has been the nature of the Bush administration since 9/11. The American response to 9/11 could have been much different. There were many other options to choose from other than a full-on military assault. Contrary to what many believe, there are ways of interpreting the Bible, Tradition, and "just war" theory that do not play into a militaristic solution. The Christian peacemaking tradition need not be equated with pacifism, but, to the pacifists' credit, they have helped us to see many other viable options of dealing with conflict before war becomes the only answer. It is tragic when Christians merge God and State, faith and allegiance to a single political party. This is just another form of Neo-Constantinianism: the seduction and subversion of the Church by the power of the State. When Christians make such a move, not only do they negate the peacemaking tradition, they also find themselves worshipping at the feet of Mars rather than Jesus.

If one peak of this Beatitude welcomes us into the Divine Life, and this Divine Life can only be lived as peacemakers in the valley of war and many injustices, the ascent to the peak on the other side of the valley affirms the fact that those who are peacemakers are the true children of God. A hawkish and ideological attitude toward life is not of God. Neither is insensitivity and indifference to human suffering. It is impossible to claim to be a child of God and not be passionately committed to justice and peacemaking. Those who claim that the Bible is their source of authority yet ignore the Beatitudes in word, thought, and deed demonstrate that the Bible is not their source of authority and that the God they claim to worship and adore is more a fiction of their making. The children of God are known as makers of peace, and they engage the world as such, but always in a non-ideological way. Such children attempt to reconcile opponents, to bring enemies together rather than widening the crevasse that separates them, lest they both fall in. This is quite a different vision than the one put forward by those who see themselves as peacemakers yet continue to perpetuate conflicts and estrangement.

It is quite natural, therefore, that the seventh Beatitude leans into the eighth Beatitude. There are serious consequences for hungering and thirsting after justice and attempting to be peacemakers in a world that either ignores such things or reduces justice and peacemaking to the politics of the right, left or centre.

Chapter Thirteen

The Prophetic Vision

The Divine Life is known by those who are persecuted for seeking Justice. Such people will know what it means to live in the Kingdom of Heaven.
Matthew 5:10

The King's good servant, but God's first.
Thomas More

The Beatitudes almost come full circle with this saying. The language of justice is raised again, but this time it is compared with the first and fourth Beatitudes in a challenging way. We return again to the notion of the Kingdom of Heaven, which means that the Kingdom that Jesus envisions is about something much more than the Kingdom of Man. Augustine's classic book, *The City of God*, sets these two Kingdoms in perspective. Those who seek justice will be filled, but they will also know the brunt of much opposition and persecution. Jesus is no silly and naïve idealist. Those who live forth the teachings of the Beatitudes will inevitably be opposed and attacked. The life of the Jewish prophets, John the Baptist, Jesus, and most of the saints and martyrs of the Church bear witness to this fact. Why should we be surprised then when we are not greeted with flowers, cheering crowds, and red carpets? This is not the welcome we are likely to receive if and when the Beatitudes are lived forth in an integrated and consistent way.

The eighth Beatitude has often been translated as, "Blessed are those who are persecuted for being righteous." Once again, within such a pietistic reading, the word "righteous" usually means some form of private and personal integrity. But the Greek word for "justice" (*dikaios*) used here is the same word used in the fourth Beatitude. In short, those who approach the meaning of justice from a Divine perspective, from the perspective of the Kingdom of Heaven will, sooner or later, collide with the Kingdom of Man. This need not always be the case, but there will be times when this conflict is the central reality. Persecution can take many forms in such situations, including outright violence and death, indifference, marginalization, and verbal or written abuse. Crises of conscience will arise, and, as in the case of Sir Thomas More, prioritized decisions will need to be made.

There are two specific words for "holiness" in Greek: *hagios* and *eusebius*. It is important to note that neither word is used in the Beatitudes to describe the person who will inherit the earth, enter the Kingdom of Heaven, be called a child of God or be filled and feasted. We hear much more about bidding *adieu* to the ego, ordering and educating our desires, thirsting for justice, being peacemakers, and being persecuted as we pursue justice. The Beatitudes do not grant us the luxury of slipping into a cheap grace, reactive religious ghettoism or sentimental and saccharine spirituality. It would have been quite possible for Matthew to use the language of *hagios* and *eusebius* to describe a person who has an integrated and mature faith, but he avoided the use of both words. This speaks much about an attitude and approach to real health, wholeness, and holiness that we do well to heed. The Divine Life consists of something much more demanding and rewarding, costly and insightful. There is no place for simplistic formulas or platitudes when we enter the fuller teachings and sayings of Jesus.

Chapter Fourteen

The Beatitudes and Prophetic Spirituality

The Divine Life is known by those who are mistreated and misun-derstood in their passion for justice. They will inherit the Kingdom of Heaven. The prophets were treated this way in the past.
Matthew 5:11–12

We mostly spend our lives conjugating three verbs: to Want, to Have, and to Do. Craving, clutching, and fussing, on the material, political, social, emotional, intellectual—even on the religious—plane, we are kept in perpetual unrest: forgetting that none of these verbs have any ultimate significance, except so far as they are transcended by and included in, the fundamental verb, to Be: and that Being, not wanting, having and doing, is the essence of a spiritual life.
Evelyn Underhill, *The Spiritual Life*

There is quite an interest in both the contemplative and prophetic interpretation of faith these days. However, an interest in the contemplative that does not engage the larger questions of the world is merely escapist and an opiate. Jesus made it clear in the final Beatitude that those who have truly heard, been informed by, and live forth his teachings will face the ire and active opposition of those in power.

There are also those who simplify the prophetic vision, domesticating and sanitizing it. Such people claim to be raising up a generation of prophets even as they ignore those issues that are at the centre of the prophetic tradition. They tend to emphasize the means of knowing as well as some of the gifts that many prophets have exercised, but they miss the deeper content, the call to character development that is the white hot fire of an authentic prophet. Those who overplay things like dreams, visions, miracles, healings, imagination, and the casting out of demons should not be dismissed or denied, but when such means of knowing or gifts of the Holy Spirit trump the bedrock teaching about the prophetic in the Beatitudes and the whole of Scripture, something of depth and substance is seriously missing.

The Beatitudes walk us straight, clean, and clear into the prophetic way, enabling us to avoid the slippery slope on either side of the prophetic path. Jesus makes this obvious in his concluding comments on the Beatitudes. We must go to such a vision if we ever hope to understand the roots of the Jewish-Christian prophetic tradition.

A good corrective to the more charismatic and renewal reading of the prophetic is a serious grounding in the Jewish oral prophetic tradition, as demonstrated in the Major and Minor prophets of the Old Testament. A deep and lengthy immersion in the Beatitudes and other books in the New Testament will only strengthen this foundation. Church Tradition can then be brought in to flesh out the fullness of such a way even further. A reading of Abraham Heschel's *The Prophets* (2001) and Walter Brueggeman's *The Prophetic Imagination* (2001) are excellent cairns to heed along the journey.

Again and again, we must make choices about our identity and life direction. We can fill our souls and time with the drugs of wanting, having, and doing. We can crave, clutch, and fuss about things that do not really matter. But there are greater depths available to us than merely chasing after the mirages that wanting, having, and doing present to us.

The publication of Martin Heidegger's *Being and Time* (1927) raised important and essential questions about how we conceptualize and live our lives. What does it mean to be? Are we merely products and victims of our times? We are thrown into time without being consulted about place, parents or a century of choice. What are we to make of this? Is our being merely an open-ended project that can be molded and shaped by social factors and personal choices? Heidegger argued that our being lacks substantive content and orientation. It does not have an ordering and forming focus. Jesus saw things quite differently, though. He shows us that our being and life direction only make sense to the degree that we allow ourselves to be open and informed by his wisdom sayings. They are a map for our new being as well as a vision of a prophetic spirituality. Those who ignore both the map and the vision miss out on the possibilities of living the Divine Life.

Verbs in the Greek language have two past tenses: aorist and imperfect. The aorist tense highlights an action done once. It is a one-time event that is now complete. The imperfect tense, on the other hand, reflects something that is done again and again. It is significant to note that the Beatitudes are written in the imperfect tense. This means that Jesus taught them often and in an ongoing and continuous way. It also means that we, as listeners, need to hear, heed, and live forth such teachings again and again.

The Beatitudes epitomize Jesus' understanding of our new Being, a Being that is meant to participate in the nature and substance of God. Our Divine Life in God is meant to be both contemplative and prophetic, a life informed by the vistas of the peaks even while it is lived in the demands of the valley. Jesus took the disciples up to the mountaintop, taught them much, and then guided them back to the lowlands to serve.

The radical and integrated vision of the Beatitudes serves as a healthy checkpoint for a Church that has often ignored such demands. The Beatitudes also offer a needful balance to Neo-Gnostics who delight in the peaks and inner life but flee from the demands of justice and peacemaking in the valley, as well as to those who wear themselves thin with such tasks but never take time out to rise above the clouds and discover the fuller existence that a more contemplative approach to life can bring. Much good can be done in the valley or on the peak, but much more good results when mountain and valley meet.

The Beatitudes lay down the trail to the peaks and the fullest scenery of life in intricate, well placed, and time-tried rip-rap steps . We are offered a vision of what it means to remember and rediscover our hidden and lost nature, which is nothing less than the image and likeness of God. This ancient yet ever new vision of our higher being calls us to see, internalize, and live forth in the valley.

Unfortunately, such a well-crafted path has it distortions, rabbit trails, and cul-de-sacs as well. The Beatitudes highlight for us an authentic prophetic way, and such a mature and timely rock rim calling is often distorted, minimized, sanitized, and domesticated. Therefore, I have concluded this missive with two appendices: one on "The Prophetic Tradition" and one on "The Neo-Gnostic Tradition" for the simple reason that there are many false prophets in our midst these days who either ignore the Beatitudes or subvert them with Gnosticism. Both approaches to spirituality demean and thin out the grand vision of Jesus in which mountains and valleys meet in a thoughtful and mature manner. Such a rip-rap path that has been laid down by the prophets and sages of old is a trail that will take us to great heights and provide discernment for life in the valley. Hence, I believe the appendices are a necessary addition and useful conclusion to this book.

The Christian Prophetic Tradition

People have understood and defined the Christian Prophetic Tradition in many ways during the history of the Church. Several sub-traditions have developed within the much larger and more epic Christian Prophetic Tradition, each with its own unique tendencies, followers, and disciples. Because none of these sub-traditions represent the complete picture (even though many of their proponents think they do), there is a desperate need to uncover, recover, and weave together the best of these prophetic traditions while also exposing their limitations and blind spots. So what are these sub-traditions? And how, at their most mature and wisest, are they part of the great tradition of the Christian prophetic way?

First, we have the "apocalyptic prophetic tradition." In this realm, a prophet is defined as one who predicts the future. Those who nod to this perspective link interpretations of the Bible to current events. Such interpretations usually point the way to the end of time, and, in its more extreme versions, support Christian-Jewish Zionism. The Jehovah's Witnesses, Seventh-Day Adventists, and variations of populist evangelical and fundamentalist Christianity often doff their dutiful caps to this understanding of the prophetic. Authors such as Hal Lindsay, William Goetz, Grant Jeffries, Jack Van Impe, and Tim LaHaye have cornered this lucrative market of interest. Frank Perreti's novels and

Michael O'Brien's *Children of the Last Days* series and *Father Elijah: An Apocalypse* also tap into this perspective.

On the positive side, this tradition does try to speak to and for those who seek to understand how God is working in and through history. However, the darker side of this notion and interpretation (mainly an evangelical right of centre tradition) was challenged soundly in a book edited by Carl Amerding and Ward Gasque called *Dreams, Visions and Oracles: The Layman's Guide to Biblical Prophecy* (1977). This collection of essays reflects the centrist and mainstream evangelical ethos. The main problem Amerding and Gasque see with the apocalyptic view of the prophetic is that it is often inaccurate. As history moves on, events inevitably disprove the predictions, thus discrediting the prophecies and those who gave them. History is littered with the wrecks of those who have bought into this agenda uncritically and been betrayed by it. Norman Cohn's *The Pursuit of the Millennium: Revolutionary Messianism in Medieval and Reformation Europe and Its Bearing on Modern Totalitarian Movements* and Katz and Popkin's *Messianic Revolution: Radical Religious Politics to the End of the Second Millennium* also speak clearly to those who are addicted to this reductionistic and one-dimensional view of the prophetic.

The second main prophetic sub-tradition is characterized by those within charismatic and renewal movements who see the prophetic mainly as personal and interpersonal words of insight or as some predicted event (and its fulfillment). The assumption is that God has spoken a direct word to the prophet for an individual, to address some situation in the life of a local congregation or to address some situation of divine significance (as defined by that particular community, of course). We can call this the "pietistic prophetic tradition." Books such as Bruce Collins' *Prophesy* or David Pytches *Some Said it Thundered: A Personal Encounter with the Kansas City Prophets* reflect this way of interpreting the prophetic. The problem with this "Word of the Lord" view is that it reduces the prophetic role to the personal or the interpersonal while ignoring the larger political, social, and economic questions that Jewish-Christian prophets always addressed. The pietistic tradition rarely bridges the personal and public domains in a meaningful or mature way. It appears to be open to God, but by reducing prophetic words merely to the personal, this sub-tradition domesticates, tames, and sanitizes the prophetic. There is no doubt that God does speak personal words, but there is much more to God's speech and action in the world than this. Prophecy may begin in the prayer closet, but it cannot stay there.

Adherents to the third prophetic sub-tradition see the prophetic mainly as a gift to the Church, calling her back to material, formal, and spiritual unity. This view of the prophetic was articulated in its finest form by J. H. Newman in his *Lectures on the Prophetical Office of the Church*. Like a prophet of old, Newman called the historic Church to remember its calling, to be rooted and grounded in the Great Tradition of old, to reunite and be one as Christ is one with the Father and the Spirit. The *unio mystica* to which Newman was so committed can be called the "ecclesiastical prophetic tradition." While this view appeals to the unity of the Church, its weakness is that it is soft on larger moral and political thought as the Church engages the world.

The fourth prophetic sub-tradition includes those who see the prophetic as, above all else, a call to justice, mercy, and peace within the Church and the World. This understanding of the prophetic is critical of a type and form of religion that reduces the life of faith to a highly charged circuit of prayer, worship, Bible study, devotionals, and church attendance but ignores the marginalized, the poor, the unborn, refugees, single parents, militarism, multi-national corporations, environmental devastation, empires, and the structural causes of poverty in our new feudal world order. Voicing the concerns of this tradition, Bishop Dom Helder Camera once said, "When I feed the poor, I am called a saint. When I ask why the poor are poor, I am called a communist." We can call this lineage the "political and liberationist prophetic tradition." It is concerned with both personal and public holiness, integrity, and authenticity. The weakness of this approach is that the political can easily be taken captive by the political perspective of the left, right or centre, and, if not careful, run roughshod over the pastoral and relational aspects of the journey.

The Christian Prophetic Tradition transcends the ethical tribalism that besets the political right, left, and centre in our era of culture wars and political correctness. At any given time, a genuine prophet may appear on the political left, in the centre or on the political right. In Canada, for example, political philosopher George Grant embodied such a consistent and integrated ethical vision of faith and prophetic insight, and he spoke such a vision in a national way. Like Grant, Milton Acorn, the "People's Poet of Canada," spoke a prophetic vision in a poetic way to his fellow Canadians. Such a perspective will seem to be on the political left when it questions things like American imperialism, corporate capitalism, environmental devastation, and structural poverty. It will seem to be on the political right when issues like the family and the pro-life agenda are defended and the gay lifestyle questioned. We need more people of Grant and Acorn's caliber to speak the public prophetic word to our excessively liberal time and ethos.

What then, in conclusion, is the Christian Prophetic Tradition? It can only be found in the meeting and merging of the four sub-traditions described above. This can only be understood in a meaningful and spiritually mature manner when we see the validity and limitations of the apocalyptic, pietistic, ecclesiastical, and political sub-traditions that have developed and how the strengths of each can compensate for the weaknesses of the others. When this linking of arms occurs, we have the true and authentic round dance of the Christian Prophetic Tradition. It is to such a round dance that the Church is called.

The Neo-Gnostic Tradition: Three Acts in an Unfolding Drama

Interest in Gnosticism has been growing clear and steady since World War II. A variety of reasons may be given for this, but the reality cannot be ignored. The present interest in Gnosticism tends to be positive rather than negative, and it is this revisionist read of the Gnostic heritage and tradition that I will touch on in this essay. This drama consists of three distinct and overlapping acts, and it is essential that each act be lived through to understand why the interest in Gnosticism continues to thrive, grow, and prosper.

Act I can be called the "discovery and scholastic phase." It began in 1945 when the Nag Hammadi Library was discovered near the Nile in Egypt. Many a decade was spent studying these ancient texts, which had been translated from Greek into Coptic. The challenging task for the scholarly community was to make such a find available to both the learned and the spiritually interested and sensitive. Translations were made, and results were published in 1977 as *The Nag Hammadi Library in English,* with an introduction by well-known Classical and Gnostic scholar James M. Robinson. Through this publication, many Gnostic texts were brought to the foreground.

In the early Church (the second to fifth centuries), Gnosticism was seen as a heresy and a heterodox movement within the larger orthodox and creedal tradition of the church. Many church fathers, both in the Bible and Patristic tradition, wrote against the Gnostic way. The discovery of the Nag Hammadi Library finally made it possible for one and all to read some of these texts that had so incited the Church's early leaders. Needless to say, there was much diversity within the Gnostic tradition, and perspectives tended to vary in depth, breadth, and insight. Missives such as *The Prayer of the Apostle Paul, The Apocryphon of James, The Gospel of Thomas, The Gospel of Philip, The Exegesis of the Soul, The Dialogue of the Savior, The Acts of Peter and the Twelve Apostles, The Gospel of Mary* and *The Testimony of Truth* are just a few of the texts in the Nag Hammadi library.

I was most interested in Act I of this unfolding drama in my undergraduate years at the University of Lethbridge for two reasons: First, we had one of the most important Gnostic scholars teaching there (Dieter Mueller). He translated two of the Gnostic texts in the Nag Hammadi Library (*The Prayer of the Apostle Paul* and *The Tripartite Tractate*). Second, I was most keen to study the Classical and Patristic phase of Christian intellectual and ecclesial history. So when the original version the Nag Hammadi texts were published in English in 1977, I was hooked. These new texts shed much light on the Late Antique and Classical phase of the Christian tradition, and publishing these missives and tracts for the times spoke much about an interest in wisdom, illumination, and enlightenment in the early Church. Now in English, the texts were there for everyone to read. But what did they mean, and what did such texts say about a period of time in western mystical and theological thought?

There were many questions to ask, and much sorting and sifting to do, but it was impossible not to read, soak, and saturate myself in the Nag Hammadi find. The 1970s were the years in which many primary, lost, and original Gnostic manuscripts became available. Needless to say, the mere fact of unearthing and translating such texts begged a deeper question: Why were such texts, thoughts, and perspectives marginalized in the Classical phase of the early Christian community? Were the Gnostics the deeper mystics and contemplatives that the Church hierarchy banished for dubious reasons? Or did the Gnostics need to be doubted and marginalized for their immature and fragmented mystical theology? These questions and many others needed to be asked and answered. I knew we could not just take the words and arguments of the apologists of centuries ago, but I also realized that bowing uncritically before the revisionist read of the Gnostics could be just as hazardous.

Act I, therefore, lasted from 1945–1977. This period of time covered the discovery of the Nag Hammadi Library (and other Gnostic texts) and the compilation and translation of such texts into English. Act II in this unfolding drama built on the discoveries of Act I and was marked by a trend toward processing and interpreting what had been discovered.

I left the University of Lethbridge in 1979 and began what became two MA degrees (at Regent College and the University of British Columbia in Vancouver, BC). Both of my MA degrees were in the area of Patristic thought in the Latin West and Greek East. I learned ancient languages and read many texts in the original tongue. The Mothers and Fathers of the Desert, the Gnostic tradition, and the contemplative and mystical theologians of the Patristic era held me near and dear. I even spent a couple of years translating many of the sayings of the Desert Mothers and Fathers, and did a course in which I had to read Gregory of Nyssa's *Life of Moses* from the Greek text. I did my first MA at Regent College on "The Spirituality of John Cassian" and my second MA (a graduating paper) on "Origen and Anthony." By this point, I had been baptized and immersed in the age and ethos of the Classical Christian tradition and the heyday of the Gnostics.

In the late 1970s and early 1980s, I began to encounter many revisionist readings of the Gnostics by the scholarly community. A major actress—Elaine Pagels—had come onto the stage, and her revisionist interpretation of the Patristic period offered a new script to ponder. There were others who antedated and anticipated Pagels, of course, but she was the new *prima donna*, reigning queen of revisionist thinking. The publication of her *The Gnostic Gospels* (1979) achieved something few scholars had been able to do in such a thorough a way (although Pagels had been leaning in such a direction in earlier publications). Most scholars of the Patristic era assumed that the Gnostics were on the edge for the simple reason that their thinking was paper-thin. There were good and solid reasons the orthodox community marginalized such heterodox mystics. Gerard Vallee (a professor of mine when I was doing my Ph.D. at McMaster in the 1980s) had written a fine book in this genre, *A Study in Anti-Gnostic Polemics* (1981). Elaine Pagels (and many other Gnostic scholars) begged to differ with this interpretation of the Gnostics. In fact, the growing scholarly Gnostic community flipped everything on its head. The Gnostics, so this new argument went, were the real saints and passionate contemplatives that the Church had mistreated. This revisionist read of the Late Antique and Patristic era garnered a growing clan and tribe. It played into a new sort of dualism, the "church is bad, spirituality is good" phenomena. The ancient Gnostics became rebel teachers and saints for the modern and postmodern spiritual seekers. The Gnostics of old rebelled against authority, patriarchy, and the constrictive nature of creeds, synods, beliefs, and institutions, as have so have many other contemporary people who have walked the mystic trail. Therefore, modern spiritual pilgrims had much in common with the ancient Gnostics. Pagels had done her revisionist read well, and it made sense to many.

It did not take much time for the next move to be made, one that suggested the real sayings of Jesus were not in the gospels. If, as the argument went, the bishops and synods dominated the drama—and they canonized the texts that reinforced their position—whom did they exclude? The sensitive and insightful Gnostics, of course! The excluded texts just might contain the deeper, secret, and real sayings of Jesus that the establishment and authoritarian structure of the Church decided to suppress. With this simple shift in thought, suddenly, the environment that spawned and embraced such works as *The Da Vinci Code* (2002) was all but in place.

This revisionist read of the Gnostics, which portrays the Gnostic writers as the real saints, masters, and mentors of the inner life, has many supporters. Pagels has written timely texts on the topic, as has Marvin Meyer, Michael Williams, Karen King, James Robinson, Hans Jonas, and Eric Voegelin (from a variety of angles). The scholarly Gnostic tribe tends to differ and deviate on what the term "Gnostic" means, the diversity of texts, and their relevance for us today, but they have definitely cornered a growing market of interest with their revisionist interpretation of the Gnostic way.

Act II in this unfolding drama continues to play itself out. The Gnostics are often idealized and romanticized in this approach, and it is hard to take some of this interpretation too seriously. As I mentioned above, I read *The Nag Hammadi Library* in the late 1970s, and the texts certainly lacked the depth, integration, and maturity of the biblical narrative and the more sophisticated reflections of the post-apostolic, early, and later Patristic contemplative and mystical way. But such a revisionist read has won the hearts and heads of many who have little or no memory of such an era. Orwell would be most pleased by all of this. It's not too difficult to convince and convert those with no memory of the past. Of course, time will clarify where and why the Gnostics and scholarly Neo-Gnostic clan has erred, but autumn and winter, perhaps, will need to come before such wisdom reappears. As it stands, the revisionist deed had been done and done well. Many were on board the ship as it left the cove and headed for the open waters.

Act III in this unfolding drama continues the tale that is being told so well. It has wooed, wedded, and bedded many. Jesus has become a Gnostic master and teacher for many, and the emerging Wisdom tradition is claiming him as its own. *The Nag Hammadi Library in English* has been updated (1990), including a new introduction by James Robinson and an afterward ("The Modern Relevance of Gnosticism") by Richard Smith. Smith's article does a superb job of putting the Gnostic tradition into a fuller, longer, and more problematic context. Robinson, on the other hand, tends to idealize the Gnostics. Marvin Meyer's recent publication, *The Gnostic Gospels of Jesus: The Definitive Collection of Mystical Gospels and Secret Books About Jesus of Nazareth* (2005) brings this drama full circle. Previously, Marvin Meyer had published *The Gnostic Bible, The Gospels of Mary: The Secret Tradition of Mary Magdalene, the Companion of Jesus, The Gospel of Thomas* and many other important books in the Gnostic genre. However, in this latest book, Meyer suggests that there are four Jesus Gnostic traditions: Thomist, Sethian, Valentinian, and Marian. The texts that reflect such traditions tell us different and divergent things about Jesus that are not in the Bible. There are the orthodox, creedal, and biblical sayings of Jesus (that do not truly tell the full and deeper truths), and there are the secret and Gnostic sayings of Jesus, which apparently take us to the heart of the matter and the man. Who is the real Jesus, therefore? Will he please stand up? Who can we trust and why are we on this revisionist trail and interpretation? Should we turn to the biblical Jesus, the Gnostic Jesus or the Jesus of the Patristic era?

Act III in this unfolding drama assumes that the real Jesus might not be in the gospel texts. Act III seeks to speak a language that is more applied and integrative, internalized and pointing in a wisdom direction. If the deeper sayings of Jesus are the Gnostic sayings, then why not hear and heed them? It is not a case of either/or, of course (biblical or Gnostic texts and sayings), but Gnostic scholars, retreat and conference leaders, and spiritual directors tend to use the Gnostic texts more and more in their teachings. Evidence of this increase in applied use of the Gnostic texts for spiritual direction and inner insight can be found in Lynn Bauman's *The Gospel of Thomas: Wisdom of the Twin* (2004). The purpose of the book cannot be missed. It includes an introduction and translation by Lynn Bauman as well as notes and questions for reflection and inquiry. Bauman builds on the work of previous scholars and applies their work to the spiritual needs and questions of our time and ethos. Bauman's conscious approach is obvious. In a rather reactionary, simplistic, and dualistic way, he contrasts the Gnostic Jesus of insight and wisdom with the colonized Jesus of the conformist, imperial, and authoritarian church of dogma and power. Such an approach will not do, and it is not worthy of a thoughtful person grounded in the literature and struggles of the Late Antique world. Bauman argues, though, that it is in *The Gospel of Thomas* that much wisdom and insight can be gleaned for our day. Apparently, Jesus passed on such hidden truths to his twin brother, and we would do well to ponder such perennial logia for our personal journey through time.

Many have followed Bauman and his Gnostic Jesus. Cynthia Bourgeault is one of then. Bourgeault has blended the insights of Bauman, Father Thomas Keating, and many others in her eclectic and Gnostic spirituality.

Books such as *The Wisdom Way of Knowing: Reclaiming an Ancient Tradition to Awaken the Heart* (2003) and *Centering Prayer and Inner Awakening* (2004) tell their own Gnostic tale and tell it well. Christopher Page, in his timely missive *Christ Wisdom: Spiritual Practice in the Beatitudes & the Lord's Prayer* (2004), also applies the thinking of Bauman and Bourgeault of Christ as a sage and master of wisdom to the Beatitudes and Lord's Prayer. Such an interpretive approach to the Beatitudes and Lord's Prayer reveals and conceals, unpacks and yet distorts the more organic, complex, and integrated notion of these central Christian sayings. Bauman, Bourgeault, and Page, therefore, are approaching Jesus as a master of insight and wisdom, and, in doing so, missing much about his concerns for justice, peacemaking, and a more political notion of the Kingdom of God. We should question this Gnostic read of Jesus when it is applied in the area of spiritual directing and conferences or retreats.

Act III, therefore, assumes that the secret and hidden sayings of the Gnostic Jesus just might have more to say to us than what we hear from Jesus in the gospels and Church Tradition. The Gnostic tradition is correct in its desire to slake a deeper spiritual thirst, but we must question whether the Gnostic Jesus can truly satisfy it.

The Classical Western Tradition of Plato, Aristotle, and the Jewish prophets (from which Jesus emerged) never separated wisdom and justice or the sage and wise person from the prophet and defender of justice and peace. Socrates and Plato challenged the Pre-Socratics' interest in metaphysics and cosmology for the simple reason that there was little or no ethical and political clout or application. The Gnostics were very much children of the Pre-Socratic and thinned-out Platonism of the Late Antique era. Plato would be appalled by the way his name was used and abused to serve perspectives he would have no interest in. Plato held high the notion of justice and the good just as the Jewish prophets did. Wisdom and justice did meet in the Classical virtues. Those who separated and divorced such lovers, as did the Gnostics, did injustice to both.

Sadly, the Church has tended to miss the deeper insights, wisdom, and justice of Jesus in the gospels, and this failure has left the spiritually hungry starving for something more. The turn we need to make today is not to the Gnostic way or the Gnostic Jesus. Instead, we need to return to the Jesus of the Sermon on the Mount, the Beatitudes, and John 14–17 for help and healing on our pilgrim way. Those who have taken the time to truly hear, meditate upon, and ponder the Jesus, the disciples, and others of the Nag Hammadi and other Gnostic texts with the Jesus of the gospels, epistles, and Church Tradition realize there were good reasons the Fathers and Mothers of the Church said a firm and solid "no" to the Gnostics.

We find little or nothing in the Gnostics texts about the centrality of justice and peacemaking, public responsibility, civic virtues and politics, ecological concerns, and the importance of place, time, and history. Most Gnostics retreated into their inner journey, elevated the spirit and the eternal while subordinating or ignoring history and time. I find it hard to take such an approach very seriously. The Jesus of the gospels and epistles is more earthbound, more of flesh and blood, more human and humane, more of the soil and stream, hawk and rock, a man of and for the people. The turn away from such a Jesus needs to be questioned today as it was in the past.

I have no doubt that Acts I–III in the ever-unfolding Gnostic drama will continue to be with us. And yet, there needs to be a counter-script written and lived out. It is this older, more integrated, holistic, and holy text that offers life and life abundant. May our hearts and minds internalize such a deeper script and speak and live the text well on the stage of life. Life on the peaks and mountains must meet and greet life in the valley and on the streets. Through the integration of such a perspective and living in the cross, chrysalis, and crucible of such a tension, we are made whole and healthy. The Gnostics (past and present) flee the tension, whereas saints are made and shaped within it. The Jesus of the Beatitudes points the way to a deeper and fuller way of knowledge and wisdom than the Gnostics of the past and present. May we turn and see such a Jesus rather than bowing and genuflecting to the thinned out Jesus of the Gnostic way.

Selected Bibliography

Augustine. *Our Lord's Sermon on the mount*. Translated by William Findlay, in the Library of Nicene and Post-Nicene Fathers, Volume 6, edited by Philip Schaeff, Grand Rapids: Eerdmans, 1974.

Barclay, William. *The Gospel of Matthew*. Burlington, Ontario: Welch Publishing Company, 1956.

Berrigan, Phil & McAlister, Liz. *The Time's Discipline: The Beatitudes and Nuclear Resistance*. Baltimore: Fortkamp Publishing, 1989.

Blanch, Stuart. *Way of Blessedness*. London: Hodder and Stoughton, 1985.

Calvin, John. *Commentary on an Harmony of the Evangelist, Mattews, Mark and Luke,* 1 (5558: Translated by William Pringle, 1845), Grand Rapids: Eerdmans, n.d.

Chrysostom, John. *Homilies on the Gospel of Matthew,* Part 1. Translated by George Prevost, Oxford, 1843.

Crosby, Michael. *Spirituality of the Beatitudes: Matthew's Challenge for First World Christians*. New York: Orbis Books, 1980.

Dart, Ron. *Erasmus and Merton: Soul Friends*. Abbotsford: Chelsea Manor Publications, 2005.

Davies, W.D. *The Setting of the Sermon on the Mount*. Cambridge: Cambridge University Press, 1964.

Eliot, T.S. *Four Quartets*. New York: A Harvest Book, 1943.

Erasmus. *Erasmus and Our Struggle for Peace*. Boston: The Beacon Press, 1950.

Frye, Northrop. *The Double Vision: Language and Meaning in Religion*. Toronto: University of Toronto Press, 1991.

Galilea, Segundo. *The Beatitudes: To Evangelize as Jesus Did*. New York: Orbis Books, 1982.

Forest, Jim. *The Ladder of the Beatitudes*. New York: Orbis Books, 1999.

Hunter, A. M. *Design for Life: An Exposition of the Sermon on the Mount*. London: SCM Press, 1965.

Jones, E. Stanley. *The Christ of the Mount: A Living Exposition of Jesus' Words as the Only Practical Way of Life*. Nashville: Abingdon, 1931.

Jeremias, Joachim. *The Sermon on the Mount*. London: Athlone Press, 1961.

Jordan, Clarence. *Sermon on the Mount*. Valley Forge: Judson Press, 1952.

Lapide, Pinchas. *The Sermon on the mount: Utopia or Program for Action?* New York: Orbis Books, 1986.

Luther, Martin. *The Sermon on the Mount:* 1521. Translated by Jaroslav Pelikan: in Volume 21 of Luther's Works. St. Louis: Concordia, 1956.

McArthur, Harvey. *Understanding the Sermon on the Mount.* New York: Harper, 1960.

Merton, Thomas. *New Seeds of Contemplation.* New York: A New Directions Book, 1961.

Merton, Thomas. *Peace in the Post-Christian Era.* New York: Orbis Books, 2004.

Rohr, Richard. *Jesus' Plan for a New World: The Sermon on the Mount.* Cincinnatii: St. Anthony Messenger Press, 1996.

Snyder, Gary. *Danger on Peaks.* Washington D.C.: Shoemaker Hoard, 2004.

Stott, John. *Christian Counter-Culture: The Message of the Sermon on the Mount.* Illinois: InterVarsity Press, 1978.

Suiter, John. *Poets on the Peaks: Gary Snyder, Philip Whalen & Jack Kerouac in the North Cascades.* Washington. D.C.: Counterpoint. 2002

Thielicke, Helmut. *Life Can Begin Again: Sermons on the Sermon on the Mount.* Minneapolis: Fortress Press, 1963.

Tolstoy, Leo. *A Confession: The Gospel in Brief and What I Believe.* Translated by Aylmer Maude in the World's Classic Series, no. 229: Oxford University Press, new edition, 1940.

Underhill, Evelyn. *The Spiritual Life.* London: Harper and Row
Publishers, 1936.

Wolin, Richard. *The Politics of Being: The Political Thought of
Martin Heidegger.* New York: Columbia University
Press, 1990.

Other Books by Ron Dart

Erasmus and Merton: Soul Friends

The Canadian High Tory Tradition: Raids on the Unspeakable

Busking

Robin Mathews: Crown Prince of Canadian Political Poets

St. Matthew's: A People's History 1900-2000 (Ed.)

Crosshairs: Being Poetic, Being Political, Being Canadian

The Red Tory Tradition: Ancient Roots, New Routes

In a Pluralist Age: Interfaith Dialogue

The Marks of the Church and Renewal

Lizard in the Palace

The Lute and the Anvil

Contemplation and the Polis

Adam: Romantics, Rationalists, Prophets: A Dialogue

About the Author

Ron Dart has taught in the department of political science, philosophy, and religious studies at the University College of the Fraser Valley since 1990. Prior to that, he worked with Amnesty International for ten years. Ron is political science advisor to the Stephen Leacock home/museum and serves on the national executive of the Thomas Merton Society of Canada. Ron has published thirteen books as well as dozens of articles, reviews, and essays. He is a frequent contributor to www.vivelecanada.ca as well as "Clarion: Journal of Spirituality and Justice" (www.clarion-journal.ca), which he also co-edits. Ron attends St. Matthew's Anglican parish in Abbotsford, BC, where he lives with his wife Karin. To learn more about Ron, please visit www.rondart.ca.